Kevin H.

AND INK BE ON THEIR HANDS

VERITAS

First published 1999 by
Veritas Publications
7-8 Lower Abbey Street
Dublin 1

Copyright © Kevin H. Donlon CSsR 1999

ISBN 1 85390 472 4

Cover design by Bill Bolger
Cover Illustration: detail from *Man Writing a Letter* by
Gabriel Metsu. Reproduced courtesy of the National Gallery
of Ireland.
Printed in the Republic of Ireland by Leinster Leader Ltd.

I have a vision and I know
The heathen shall return.
They shall not come with warships,
They shall not waste with brands,
But books be all their eating,
And ink be on their hands.
G. K. Chesterton

The Ballad of the White Horse

ACKNOWLEDGEMENTS

The works listed below are gratefully acknowledged by the author, who makes reference to them in his text.

The Stature of Waiting, W. H. Vanstone (Darton, Longman & Todd).

Memory Hold-the-Door, John Buchan (Hodder and Stoughton).

Dunkerrin: A Parish in Ely O'Carroll, Seamus Ó Riain (Dunkerrin History Committee Publishers).

Old-Fashioned Pilgrimage and Other Poems, Austin Clark (The Dolmen Press).

Small Net In A Big Sea, Michael Baily.

Philippine Literature: A Twofold Renaissance, Miguel Bernard SJ.

A Priesthood in Tune, Thomas Lane (Columba Press).

Tensions: Necessary Conflicts in Life and Love, H. A. Williams (Mitchell Beazley).

Introducing The Christian Life, Michael Ramsey (SCM Press).

St Thomas More, Richard Marius (London: J. M. Dent & Son).

A Moment of War, Laurie Lee (Viking).

The RCs, George Scott.

Media in Ireland: The Search For Diversity, Damien Kiberd (ed.) (Open Air Press).

New Hearts for New Models: A Spirituality For Priests Today, Daniel J. O'Leary (Columba Press).

FOREWORD

There is an old saying which anyone attempting 'to put something down on paper' should remember. It goes: 'No tears in the writing, no tears in the reading.' I did not have this worry particularly in mind when I wrote these pages but there were tears, mostly of frustration! I hope the reader has fewer of them than I had.

I do want to say two things. Firstly, about the format of this book. The original idea (to which I held) was very simple. I wanted to put down in some clear form the many ideas and concepts and promptings which had come to me over the years: ideas on education, preaching, teaching, writing, the media, especially the Church media, the Church itself, the renewal, the missionary ideal, books, suffering, celibacy and on and on. Were I to deal with these ideas in an abstract way I should write a book nobody could read. Were I to insert these ideas into a more traditional autobiographical form I should be attempting a book I could not write. I was stuck.

Then I got the break. I came on a lovely book called *Warrenpoint* by the very distinguished literary critic and teacher, Professor Denis Donoghue. It was for me a godsend. While being autobiographical and fairly chronological, the book did not have chapters. It had short sections and sub-sections. These sections dealt with all the beliefs and ideas which had preoccupied the author over many years. The sections were brief and tempting to read, and when put together presented a fair picture of things. I felt I could follow this format, which would be easy for me and for the reader. I had been a magazine editor for twenty-one years and had to re-write thousands of articles of about a thousand words. I myself had written many articles of about the same length. It was the way I should go.

The second thing I want to say is that when I had finished this book I discovered to my surprise that I had left out, almost totally, the one dimension of living which means most to me after my faith. I had left out my friends. Apart from a few references to friendship in the context of celibacy or prayer, I had said nothing about those dear to me. Why? It may be that I was not able to put into words how I felt. Perhaps that strange and wonderful silence which wraps friends around as they walk together through life had stolen into my heart or pen. I have always had the feeling somewhere deep inside that sharing a valued treasure – a person, a book, a poem, an experience – does some kind of damage to the treasure, takes something of the sheen or shine off it.

Whatever the reason, the thing is done. In apology I dedicate these pages to my friends, and stand by the words of Belloc (though in old age he regretted having written them):

> *From quiet homes and first beginning*
> *Out to the undiscovered ends*
> *There is nothing worth the wear of winning*
> *But laughter and the love of friends*

K. H. Donlon
12 May 1997

6

As I begin the task of writing these pages, I question my motives for doing so. Why do I bother? Well, for one thing, it will probably be best for my health if I do. It has been knocking or hammering about inside me for a long time now. If something must be born it must.

There is a compulsiveness about writing itself. Few people realise that it can be an addiction. To call great names in support: Graham Greene said that he simply had to have, always, a book in the making. Somerset Maugham felt, when he could no longer hold a pen, that a great driven burden had been lifted from his shoulders. On a humbler plane, after twenty-one years of editing a magazine, writing and re-writing a great deal, I too feel the touch of compulsion. As the Scots poet William Soutar put it: 'Once a scribbler, always a scribbler'.

But there is more to it than that. Sometimes a single remark illustrates a whole world. Last year I attended the golden jubilee of ordination of an old friend. There were speeches and toasts, and then it was over. As we sat chatting together that night, he said, as if talking to himself: 'Fifty years of what I have known and felt and been through all reduced to this!' He paused for a moment and then got up, as if dismissing his thoughts, but managed to add, with some bitterness, I felt, 'He was a great full-forward in football!' I remember thinking how dreadful it must be to feel that one's whole life should be summed up in a few throwaway remarks on one's sporting prowess of long ago.

But what of all that had happened between the long ago and now? All the times he had changed someone for the better, all the preaching and anointing, all the caring and the hope, all the smiles and the thanks and the rejections, all the nights he had sat through with an old dying woman who had no one else to sit by her side, all the graves he had stood by, especially those of children, the morning he held in each arm the young husband and wife as the three looked down on the lovely boy of five dead from meningitis, all the loneliness, all the times he fell in love, the day still present in his memory when the most wonderful girl he had ever met told him that she had fallen in love with him, all the times for so long afterwards when he felt the tears, all the days and nights when he just held on, not able to resort to prayer or counsel or grace, or even, it seemed, God, but just sheer bloody holding on – the mention of the place of his worst desolation still bringing it back, but he did hold on. Paul's words about being poured out on the altar had a resonance in his memory: he too could say, diffidently perhaps and from far behind, 'I have run the great race, I have finished the course, I have kept the faith!'

My friend was right: we are not being human when we reduce another's life to a goal scored in a lost summer. But we do it and we are not always to blame. How can our story be told or known unless we tell it, or better still write it? Though writing seems to carry a strange horror for so articulate and talented a group of men as the clergy. Maybe somewhere deep down they know that another pen is writing elsewhere. Maybe the lines of R. S. Thomas on the country clergy are nearer the mark:

> *They left no books,*
> *Memorial to their lonely thought*
> *In grey parishes; rather they wrote*
> *On men's hearts and in the minds*
> *Of young children….*

I think it is Cyril Connolly (in *Enemies of Promise*) who claims that people write books to meet the deep desire in all of us to be immortal. There are easier ways, I would have thought. However, before we achieve immortality, a little mortality comes in useful. The vast majority of writers, in fact, have written to survive, to keep the wolf from the door; as Patrick Kavanagh might have put it, 'to earn a chop for supper', or as Dr Johnson said, 'No man but a blockhead ever wrote except for money'.

Perhaps the simplest and most natural of all reasons for writing one's story is expressed in the everyday phrase 'packing our bags'. On a parish mission in Dublin's York Street, I came upon a lovely old woman who was the last of her line. 'I am very happy now,' she said, 'I have everything tidied up. I have paid for my funeral and for all the arrangements. I am content!' Anyone who works with the elderly will tell you that a person's deepest need in the end is to tidy up: their thoughts, their effects, their hearts. Then they go easily. They have packed their bags.

🐾 🐾 🐾

'I am an endless seeker,' declared Emerson, 'with no past at my back.' It is hard to accept that an intelligent man could have thought that way. One has only to experience someone who has lost his or her memory: they are truly lost, mystified, helpless, and all around them are helpless too. As an old Red Indian proverb put it, 'Without memories we are as wind to the buffalo grass.'

And a collective loss of memory is as serious for an institution or the Church as the personal individual loss. Many forms of the great Renewal in the Church following Vatican II went astray because we had forgotten our past; sometimes we had, quite simply, forgotten our very theology.

There is something deep in human nature which wants to go on reinventing the wheel. Avery Dulles wrote in *The Resilient Church:* 'Reformers are not revolutionaries, they do not intend to destroy and recreate. They are moderates who respect the integrity of that which they are seeking to refashion.' Jesus said, 'I have not come to destroy the law but to fulfil it.'

How far back can or should one remember? The question often results in amusing stories or claims. I don't know if anyone takes seriously the assurance of Henry James (*A Small Boy and Others*) that he remembers as a baby, in long clothes, standing on the lap of someone in a carriage as it drove down the rue St Honoré in Paris. He was even then 'impressed' at seeing the beautiful Place de Vendôme with its great column at the centre. It is a wonder he did not join the travel books and tell us that the column was encircled by a band of bronze made from 1200 cannons captured by Napoleon at Austerlitz!

I can certainly remember an event, when I was seven, which is no achievement at all. It was an event which left a deep mark on the folk memory of the nation: the Eucharistic Congress in 1932. I can remember clearly hearing John McCormack singing the Panis Angelicus on the wireless from the Phoenix Park. It was not that I could appreciate the matchless voice, but my brother and myself had been told to listen: our parents were there at the Mass.

I can also remember another event which took place well before that, a much-talked-about celebration. I had often wondered what it was. It was the Centenary of Catholic Emancipation in 1929. I was then four years old, having begun school at the age of three.

In more than one way 1925 was a lucky year for me. As I am virtually unable to add or subtract it is handy to have begun life with a figure ending in five; one can add forward fairly safely in fives! The year 1925 always catches my eye on a page. Hitler published *Mein Kampf* in 1925, Mussolini became dictator of Italy that year: the storm was already brewing. F. Scott Fitzgerald published his famous novel *The Great Gatsby* in 1925, a year which also saw the birth of another enduring book by a man who has brightened many lives: *Carry on, Jeeves* by P. G. Wodehouse.

I am not well up on the history of popular songs but one of the most durable of them arrived that year too: 'Show Me the Way to go Home.'

🐜 🐜 🐜

It is said that 'people are places'. Once a loved one dies the place is never the same. After the death of his beloved wife, Harold Nicolson, author of the greatest modern diary in English, could never again visit a place where he had been with her.

As for myself, I have a particular affinity with actual houses. For example, I loved the college building of St Clement's in Limerick where I was a boarder as a boy. When I moved on to become a novice in St Joseph's in Dundalk I found I hated the house. Incidentally, I was very unhappy there also, though the two things did not always go together. I have been extremely happy for over twenty years in my present home, Marianella, though I have no love whatever for the actual house itself. I lived for six marvellous years in St Clement's College in Iloilo in the Philippines and the house there has a special place in my memory; but another seven memorable years in Cebu left me with no warm feelings at all for the building itself.

Where does all this come from? I believe it comes from my relationship with the house in which I was born, Birchgrove.

By any standards it was an unusual house. The most striking feature of the building was a broad round tower with an onion-shaped top. It was a piece of architecture which served no real purpose. From inside, when you reached the top steps of the stairs leading to the fourth floor, you saw that the tower was completely hollow. In fact it was the top of the well of the stair-case, the stairs being beautifully spiral. We four brothers polished the steps of that endless stairs many times, but mostly we thundered up and down them, getting louder as we grew older and heavier. The kitchen was a vast space, with its ceiling spattered with small hooks, for hanging and drying meat, I presume. For us it was the perfect stage-set for the most glorious Christmas decorations: holly, buntings, streamers. In the corner was a Benn and Wellwood range which produced a good fire from the hard, black turf of Monahincha bog. To give some idea of the odd shape of the house, the kitchen was at ground level, but on going up one flight of stairs you came to the sitting-room, which was (almost) on ground level too.

It is that sitting-room which, before everything else, holds a special place in my memory. It was, quite simply, the most beautiful room I ever saw. Even as boys growing up (not the most beauty-conscious people in the world) we used to bring visitors proudly to it. One side of the room held a giant bay-window and to reach it you had to step through four or five rows of my mother's flowers and ferns. The colours of the curtains on either side are still as clear in my memory as if it were yesterday – and I have been in that room only once in the last forty years. The room had been, I believe, a ballroom (it was that big), but its crowning glory was the furnishings: the carpets, the armchairs, the silver, the piano, the pictures. Both my parents had marvellous taste in matching colour and shape.

A few days ago I spoke on the phone to my youngest brother. He is now in his fifties. I asked him if he had heard some rumour that that lovely room had been divided up or partitioned by its present owners. His reply was immediate: 'Oh no,' he said, 'that would be a barbarism!'

When I was in third-level education, as a major seminarian, I attempted to write an essay on that house of ours. (It was not, by the way, 'our house' in the sense of our owning it. We were tenants.) In the piece I tried to give some idea of what my memory of the house was like. I remember talking about the jackdaws. They haunted the place. The raucous call of any member of the crow family, the jackdaw, the magpie or the crow, has been ever since for me the most nostalgic of sounds. But my memory's picture of Birchgrove was set against a larger memory: the rambling outhouses, the lake, the scuttling water-hens, the squirrels, and very specially the swallows and swifts. I can remember clearly looking out from my bedroom window on a late summer evening and seeing the swallows race along a foot or two from the ground, as they collected insects for their numerous young in the mud nests high up under the eaves. One evening in that room, while it was still bright day, I recall feeling lonely for the first time. I had just finished reading *Robin Hood* and felt lost at parting with my new friends from the green glades of Sherwood. It was the very beginning of my love of books.

But to come back to my essay: it was ill received, certainly not appreciated, and nothing approaching encouragement was hinted at. Had I, later, as a teacher of English for eleven years, found anything near such a memory recall in one of my own students, anything at all like it, I should have been delighted. But not so in the thinking or atmosphere of what passed for an education process in the major seminary of that time.

'He was wholly without ambition. He did not know the meaning of class-consciousness; he would have stood confidently before kings and was quite incapable of deferring to anybody except the very old and the very poor. He was not, I suppose, the conventional saint, for he was not over-much interested in his own soul. But he was something of the apostle and, if it be virtue to diffuse a healing grace and to lighten the load of all who cross your path, then he was the best man I have ever known.'

So wrote the author John Buchan (*Memory-Hold-the-Door*) of the Calvinist minister who was his father. He did however add, 'My father had about as much diplomacy as a rhinoceros.' In many ways those words remind me strongly of my own father, with one exception: he was supremely a man of peace. When his brother, my uncle John, died, a cousin said to me, 'You know, if John were struck in the face he would actually turn the other cheek.' So would my father. And to add to the peace, my father was also (and nobody who knows me will believe it) an extremely silent man. Both of us liked walking but he would walk for hours without a word. Only one of his sons inherited that silence.

In our world today of psychedelic dress where, especially among some, there is almost a cult of ugliness, I cannot even imagine my father casually dressed. I never saw him walk a step in shirt sleeves or in slippers or unshaven. He indulged almost in a cult of cleanliness – his full suit, shirt and tie always matching. He was ready for the day when, fully dressed, he checked his watch and polished his glasses. A final touch (which I remember especially from summer time), he would tap the weather glass to see how things were outside.

Being in the law business he tended to use many of the forms of address of that trade. Until remonstrated with by my mother he used to address priests as 'Sir'. Once when he called to see me in boarding school I was mortified to hear him so address the Director, but I was comforted later by the same Director who said: 'Don't worry, Kevin, law men speak that way.'

Although he was much more demonstrative than my mother in expressing his regard for his sons, he still, in his letters, kept to dry formal phrases. I have beside me a letter from him dated 25 September 1957. I had obviously asked him (from the Philippines) to find two pictures for me. It begins: 'My dear Kevin, Further to my Lr. of Monday please see the enclosed Lr. from M/S Gill & Son that they have no difficulty with Our Lady's picture but the other – St Aloysious – is only 10x7 inches. I have written them to send you the two etc.' However the letter ends with 'God bless you always and your great work. Write me when you get this. With fondest love, Daddy'.

Sometimes, in his letters, he would refer to a third person with the very legal expression 'the other party'. And he always caused me to smile with a sentence like 'It is no trouble at all, my dear fellow, to do this for you'.

Have I inherited anything from my father? One thing certainly: impatience. My father was the most impatient person I ever met. He became restless, questioning and gesturing if he had to wait a moment. He was never late for anything and nobody else had better be late either. I can still see him, walking up and down on a Sunday morning, slapping his gloves from one hand to the other and beckoning to the rest of us to hurry up and be out to Mass. This was fifteen minutes before any reasonable time of departure. If you indulged in any gesture or phrase or stance which he did not like he pounced immediately.

In writing about my father I would not dare to write in reproach. He was too good a man for that. But he was contradictory. He had an immense admiration for anyone who was, as he would say, 'good at his job', and yet he himself had no personal ambition whatsoever. He did not, for example, progress at all in his own profession. He was, at the same time, a great student and reader, indeed liked reading to others. The Essays of Macaulay were a favourite. One can even detect some of the rhythms and balances of that famous style in the letters which my father wrote, now and then, to the papers. Dickens was another favourite of his, as were, strangely, all the works of Sir Arthur Conan Doyle.

History, however, was his great love. He read widely on the Reformation and the Counter-Reformation. Growing up in the shadow of two wars (the Boer War and the Great War) he was always fascinated by their history. Once two of my brothers took him, in later life, on a drive through the battlefields of Northern France. They were amazed at the specific details and knowledge which he demonstrated at particular points. He belonged to the generations which were deeply scarred by the experience of the First World War. Even for men now nearing their hundredth year, the ghosts of Ypres and the Somme seem to be always passing by. Leaving aside (if possible) the two sister nightmares of Nagasaki and the Holocaust, many will agree that, for all its terrors, the Second World War has not touched the lives of those who lived through it in anything like the same terrible way as did the Great War.

My father carried for years in his prayer book the mourning card of Bishop Hoare of Ardagh and Clonmacnoise. He had often, as a young man, heard him preach in St Mel's Cathedral in Longford, where my father was born. It was the high moment in his memory of everything which, in later life, he came (a little pompously) to praise in the Church: its ceremony, its colour, its authority, its sense of the past. He did not live to see or hear the avalanche of criticism – good and bad – which now falls frequently upon the so-called institutional Church. I fear he would be very short of sympathy with most of it.

For many years my father was a daily communicant and would readily discuss spirituality, including his own. Once I had to refuse when he asked to borrow a book from our community library. One did not lend books then – nor should one now! The book was a famous one: *Trust in God* by Paul de Jaeger SJ. The request was a little light thrown on the spiritual life of a thoughtful Christian.

My father died on 20 March 1965. He was seventy-six. I was in the Philippines and could not attend his funeral. Writing to me afterwards, my brother Brendan, in whose parochial house he died, said: 'He died a most peaceful death, serene and content as you would expect. I have never seen so clearly as in his death the truth of the saying "as a man lives so shall he die: What things soever a man shall sow those also will he reap".'

The old man had a form he always used in saying goodbye: 'God be with you.' It is a prayerful wish I do not need to express now; I am certain he is with God.

🐜 🐜 🐜

One of the very first poems I learned by heart has remained with me. Mainly, perhaps, because my mother liked it and used to join in when she heard it recited. It was 'The Passing of the Gael' by Ethna Carbery.

> *They are going, going, going for the valleys and the hills,*
> *They are leaving far behind them heathery moor and*
>   *mountain rills,*
> *All the wealth of hawthorn hedges where the brown*
>   *thrush sways and thrills.*

Ethna Carbery, whose real name was Anne Johnston Mac Manus, was a Belfast woman. She spent the last few years of her short life in Donegal. Her fame rests on just one volume of poems, *The Four Winds of Erin*, published shortly after her death in 1902. She should be called the Poet of the Exile but is now almost forgotten. Though not completely: she made a fitting, brief appearance at a moving moment in modern Irish history. When John F. Kennedy, President of the United States, addressed the Houses of the Oireachtas in 1963 he quoted her. Representing the great Republic which had given a home to countless thousands of emigrants over the generations, and being himself the son of exiles, it was only right that he should quote 'The Passing of the Gael'. As he said slowly, in his Boston accent, the line 'They are going, going, going and we cannot bid them stay', I wonder how many who heard him knew the source?

My mother would have known it. She was a national school teacher, a graduate of the famous Training College of Carysfort, now sadly no more. Both she and her sister were called to training in the same year. One of her teachers was Éamon De Valera (indeed she attended his last class before the 1916 Rising). She retained a great admiration for him and would always have voted on his side; something my father would never have done!

It is easy to write about particular persons: people are so varied, so complex, so rich, so bad, so good. Except when writing about one's mother. It is often only in later life, when she is gone, that one comes to see her objectively. At least this is how it is with me. My mother was a very private person, even within her family. She talked only about certain areas of her past, one of them being her years in the secondary school in Carrick-on-Shannon run by the Marist Sisters. She loved the sisters. She was very proud of Carysfort and never had the remotest touch of the bitterness or complaint which marks the memories of so many people now when they talk of nuns. As a young teacher she taught in the Sacred Heart Convent in Roscrea and her experience there was the same.

My mother was a very tense person, due mainly, I think, to the circumstances of her own upbringing. She was certainly a great worrier, something she passed on to her family. But she was not a gloomy person, in fact she was very good humoured, a great mimic and absolutely marvellous when reading stories. She used to read *Our Boys* for us (Kitty the Hare: Victor O D'Power) and take off all the characters in the plot. Some of her sons have a certain amount of dramatic talent. It came from her.

Like most Irish families my mother's family was mixed. There were RIC on both sides but there were republican connections too. Great pride was taken in one member of the family, going back 175 years. He is mentioned by name in John Keegan Casey's poem 'The Rising of the Moon 1798'.

> *'Oh, then tell me Shaun O Ferrall,*
> *Tell me why you hurry so?'*
> *'Hush, ma buchal, hush and listen.'*
> *And his cheeks were all aglow.*
> *'I bear orders from the Captain –*
> *Set you ready quick and soon:*
> *For the pikes must be together*
> *At the rising of the moon'.*

Being a teacher, my mother spoke Irish well and took us for many a summer to the lovely Gaeltacht in Ring, Co. Waterford. My father came now and then but was rather out of place. He had, literally, only one word of Irish and it amused him endlessly, why I don't know.

My mother's sympathies were all nationalist and Gaelic. She gave Irish names to all her sons: Brendan, Kevin, Aidan,

Aengus. I remember clearly the day Douglas Hyde was made first President under the new Constitution. She sat us down next day in the kitchen and read out all about it from the papers.

I was taught by my mother only very briefly but she was a good teacher – if one is to go by the countless comments I heard as I gave missions later in the Killaloe diocese. She was principal of Emmel National School in Dunkerrin parish and many times, after confession, I got 'Father, your mother taught me in Emmel. She was a lovely teacher.'

Just thinking about my mother, there is one thing which puzzles me. She liked people and got on well with them. She had very good judgement and gave it freely, to clergy included. When priests came to her school promoting vocations to the missionary life she was very helpful. She was a great letter-writer and was consulted by the extended family. And yet, with a few special exceptions, she did not like visitors to our home. She certainly did not preside over an open house! Later, after I had gone on to the major seminary, things changed a little and my younger brothers brought their friends to our home. The only explanation I can give for this is that she came from an RIC family and, I believe, such families tended to stay a little apart and not mix much socially with others, for various reasons.

Unlike my father, my mother never talked about her spiritual life. She had a great devotion to the Little Flower but, after that, was very matter-of-fact about religion. When I started as a young priest on parish missions I used to feel a little embarrassed (within myself) when advocating the family Rosary. We never said it at home. In the month of May my mother built a little altar to Our Lady in the house and we said the Rosary each day that month. But that was all. She saw three sons ordained and the fourth a deacon before she died but she never made a deal about this or anything approaching a boast. She never pressed any of us or suggested that we might go on for the priesthood. If we did, that was good. She did, of course, give encouragement once we were on the way but no more. Our vocations were certainly not 'mother's vocation'. That this happens sometimes is a fact, but not, I believe, to the extent often claimed.

That matter-of-factness of hers extended to her relations with my father. Years after both of them were with God I once said to a brother of mine, 'Did you ever notice that she never praised Father?' He replied, 'Maybe, but then I should not like to be around if anyone said anything against him in her presence.'

On the morning of 2 June 1959, as I was going into breakfast in the Philippines, an old friend, Fr Michael Coffey, handed me a cable. 'This has just come in, Kevin,' he said. Holding on to it he added, 'They never cable good news. I'll open it for you.' It read: 'Mother died suddenly last night. Brendan.'

There was a prayer she used to say in school every day about 'an unprovided death'. I know it was answered. But she died alone in her sleep, alone in the house. All her sons were in exile, in the service of the Church, it is true, but still far away. I often wonder if she had not had some intuition about this as she recited, long ago, the poem that seemed to have some hold on her: 'They are going, going, going from the valleys and the hills...shy-eyed colleens and lads so straight and tall.'

※ ※ ※

When I mention to people, just in the course of conversation, that I was not able to be present at either my father's or my mother's funeral I often get the response: 'Isn't that dreadful?' or 'Isn't that inhuman?'. I do not think so, actually. It was at the time, of course, an experience I cannot put in words, but I did soon, gratefully, come to see it in perspective. When dealing with the past we have to understand it on its own terms. Otherwise history is nonsense, an exercise in hindsight. People acted in the past within their limitations, by the light of what they saw then, not by our lights now.

In the past, many if not most missionaries went to the foreign missions for life, as did the early Redemptorists to the Philippines. It was thought best. It was hard but accepted. Later on the term was reduced to ten years, in my time to seven. There were, too, the geographical facts. Before air travel the journey from Manila to Dublin took five weeks – not too helpful when thinking of being in time for a funeral!

I have seen confrères, Fathers and Brothers, anguished, bitter with 'a chip on their shoulder' all their lives because of something which they had to endure in the past which would not be allowed to happen now. It is a great folly to allow the past to dictate to us the kind of people we are or should be today. But that is what is happening. Even for a repose of mind and heart it is good to accept the difference between the past and the present. It is not easy. The great historian Arnold Toynbee said that one of the central mistakes of history was to keep fighting the battles of today with the weapons of yesterday.

I have been asked more than once where I found my keen interest in ecumenism. I do remember, as a major seminarian, saying religiously every year, the prayers of the Chair of Unity Octave (18-25 Jan) These prayers had their origins in an

Episcopalian group of Religious, the Society of the Atonement, founded at Graymoor, forty miles north of New York. The eight days' prayer was first celebrated in 1908 but the following year the Society became Catholic and brought the Octave with them into the Roman Catholic Church. It has since become worldwide and that week has become a focal point every year for ecumenical activity within and among the Christian Churches.

But that is not exactly where my interest in ecumenism began or rather where the seeds were sown. Those seeds were sown by my experience of Church of Ireland neighbours. The house where we lived was owned by the Reid family, who occupied the larger half of the big rambling complex which was Birchgrove. Mr and Mrs Reid (always Mr and Mrs) and Noel and Mary were Protestant, but our two families were very close. We were open house to each other. As young people we shared games and books and birthdays. As we grew up and went our ways the ties remained. I have before me a photo of my youngest brother's ordination and I see Mr and Mrs Reid smiling in the group. My brother Brendan and I helped to take the memorial service of both of those two wonderful Christian people. We remained close to the late Noel who lived in Kildare and to Mary who lives in Britain.

These simple facts do not, of course, give any idea of my feeling (and that of my brothers) for the Reid family. We loved them. What we experienced was not just friendly neighbours but eminently good people. Nobody can live comfortably with the idea of divided Christians if one sees and feels, at close quarters, the goodness, the uprighteousness, the fidelity to their faith of people whom we are now asked to call 'separated brethren'. Cardinal Newman was right when he said 'the division of Churches is the corruption of hearts'.

I notice on visits to my two brothers in England (who are parish priests) the ease with which they relate to the local

Church of England rector and his family. I know exactly where it comes from. Not so long ago Mary Reid, who is now retired from nursing, told me of her taking Cardinal Heenan (years ago) on a look-around of her hospital. As they were parting, the cardinal asked her: 'Where did you get your ease talking to a Roman Catholic archbishop?' She replied, 'I am Irish and grew up with four priests-to-be who have remained my friends. I think I got it there.'

When preaching on ecumenism I tend to stress three things. The very first ecumenical gesture asked of all of us is that we be good, upright, worthy members of our own faith tradition. You will always notice that it is the utterly good and saintly people in each tradition who are most enthusiastic for ecumenism.

Secondly, we must know our own faith well. The great enemy of ecumenism is ignorance – of others and of ourselves. We can only dialogue from within our own Church beliefs if we know those beliefs, understand them reasonably, are at home with them, can articulate them. This alone will give us the confidence, the 'repose', the 'room' to be able to listen to others, to hear and feel what they are saying and feeling.

Thirdly, we must work, each one, to find within ourselves a deep awareness of the real tragedy of the division of the Churches. Christianity will be more divided in the approaching year AD 2000 than it was in the year 1000. And we are all to blame. The great German poet Novalis described the Reformation break, in the sixteenth century, as 'the mortal sin of Christianity'. We cannot emphasise too often the basic truth from St John's Gospel: without the unity of the Christian Church the world will not believe that Jesus Christ is who he is, nor will it believe in the loving Fatherhood of God.

This is merely to mention the steps, as it were, towards our understanding and fulfilling of the Unity movement. But the best start of all must surely be, as it was for me, getting to know and love good people of another persuasion. One then begins to feel, long before one begins to know, that we are actually undivided in the loving heart of a loving God.

🐜 🐜 🐜

I first learned the haunting lines of T. W. Rolleston in Cloneganna National School.

> *In a quiet water'd land, a land of roses*
> *Stands St Kieran's city fair;*
> *And the warriors of Erin in their famous generations*
> *Slumber there*
> *There they laid to rest the seven Kings of Tara,*
> *There the sons of Cairbré sleep –*
> *Battle-banners of the Gael, that in Kieran's plain of crosses*
> *Now their final hosting keep.*

Cloneganna school was in the parish of Dunkerrin, Co. Offaly, on the borders of Tipperary – T. W. Rolleston country. Passing through the little village of Dunkerrin you see the famous Rolleston arches outside the Protestant Church, built there by Frances Rolleston in 1757 for the convenience of vendors attending the great fairs of the time.

T. W. Rolleston was himself a distinguished scholar. His poem 'The Dead of Clonmacnoise' is from the Irish of Angus O'Gillan. The Rollestons were originally Norman. They came with the first Planters to Ulster and later acquired lands in Limerick and Tipperary.

In his very interesting book *Dunkerrin: A Parish in Ely O'Carroll*, Séamus Ó Riain publishes a photo of Cloneganna National School, built in 1845. It stands there desolate and forlorn and long since closed; but not in my memory. I had previously attended Corville School in Roscrea parish where I made my First Communion, prepared by a loved teacher, Mrs Meagher, but my national school was Cloneganna. There I made my first friends, among them the late Fr Tom and Fr John Comerford, Sister Mary and the late Sister Susie Teehan. It was there I bought my first hurley and began a love of hurling which has stayed with me ever since. In so far as I can recognise myself, I began in Cloneganna.

When one gives thought to our national schools, especially before they were modernised, one can only admire their achievement. Cloneganna school was just four walls, literally. There were desks and a fireplace, but nothing much else: no lighting, no water, no heat (pupils brought sods of turf with them), no recreation space worth talking about, no partitioning of one teacher's area from another, 'dry toilets' outside, a few hooks inside for coats and caps. That was it.

And yet we learned a great deal, to read and write reasonably for one thing. Some achievement in today's world when a university professor, Michael Dummett, has just been driven to write a book *Grammar and Style for Examination Candidates*. That is, third-level students! In Cloneganna I began to get a sense of our history, of the past, of geography, of local literature and lore, of books, of politics.

I remember quite clearly one particular day sitting on the running board of my mother's car (cars don't have them now) and reading the daily paper avidly. I was twelve. It was after school and must have been 15 March 1938. Hitler had carried off the Anschluss, the unification of Germany and Austria. On the previous Saturday evening he had crossed the Austrian frontier at his birthplace, Braunau. Three hours later he was in Linz on the Danube. Next morning he laid a wreath at the grave of his parents in Leonding and then set off on his triumphant drive across Austria – the paper was full of the delirium, the cheers, the flowers, the flags. On the following day, 14 March, Hitler entered Vienna. Addressing the massed crowds from the balcony of the Hofburg he declared: 'As Führer and Chancellor of Germany I hereupon report to history the entry of my homeland into the Reich.'

There was one small item of equipment the national schools did have: maps. There was Ireland, the world, Europe. From early on we got a sense of where we were. Not a bad start from more than one point of view. The isolationism, the provincialism, the ignorance which now plague our approach to some of the world's problems have their origins in simple geography. Or rather the lack of it.

In looking back, of course, one has to be careful. Have I commented on the national schools with the help of nostalgia? If one's experience in the past has been, in general, happy, one tends to do some rose-tinting. If one's experience has been unhappy one tends to darken the shadows. All I can honestly say is this: when I went to secondary school in 1938 I was joined by twenty other young students, all from national schools, town and country. I did not feel remotely superior to them, nor was I, in either education or general information. In fact, the opposite was true. Many of them had already started on subjects of which I knew nothing. They were easily as informed on things as I was, as good at reading, writing, arguing. Much as I have to thank my teachers in Cloneganna (Mrs Barry and Mrs Duggan), I do have to say that they were not an exception. Our national schools of the 1930s and 1940s can, in general, hold their heads high.

      🐜 🐜 🐜

The journalist John Horgan has said that talking about education in Ireland is like hurling rockets into a black hole in space; it is the last you hear of them. Not so any longer I suspect, but still, as a subject of interest or concern education does have its problems. Those who have experience of something approaching the real thing are the luckiest. I feel I was one of them.

I went to the Redemptorist Secondary School in Limerick in 1938. It is now St Clement's College. About ten years ago, on the occasion of its century, I wrote a piece for the centenary book. I would not have any reason to change anything I said then:

> The Director of the college was Fr John E. Treacy, known to generations of us as Fr Jack. Although he has been the source and subject of countless stories and jokes and mimicry across the years he remains for me (and I suspect for many others) one of the most influential people in my life. Fr Jack had marvellous ideas on education. To him it was not an activity confined to the classroom or the examination paper or the making of a living. In spite of being as a person dismissive and intolerant, very predictable in all his reactions, he had the broad view. He had vision. He did want to see young people going from the college who had confidence in themselves, who could speak well and clearly, who had an interest in music and literature, who knew something about the arts such as painting and sculpture, who knew that reading added to the joys of living, who knew that our own country was not the universe and yet have a deep love and feel for it, who knew that external appearances in dress and table manners and general courtesy were somehow very important. In a word Fr Jack Treacy knew something of what education is about. He did believe that every student should get this start in life, have sown seeds in his heart and mind which could flower in later years into a reasonably rounded and cultured person.

I believe that Fr Jack Treacy could have written the statement published as in 1997 by the Conference of Major Religious Superiors: 'The fundamental purpose of education is to enable individuals to grow towards their unique potential for wholeness and, at the same time, to promote a sense of citizenship and social solidarity which are prerequisites for the worthwhile development of the nation.'

* * *

One of the pitfalls in talking about education is falling into the trap of the lofty statement, the grand ideal. It can be very different on the ground. What was it like on the ground for us? St Clement's College at that time had only sixty students and it is interesting now to recall what we did. Each year we put on an English play, an Irish play and a light opera. The English play was always Shakespeare. In my six years we presented *Coriolanus, Hamlet, As You Like It, Twelfth Night, A Midsummer Night's Dream* and *The Tempest*. Only one of these (*Hamlet*) was a prescribed examination text. Shakespeare was on the boards to give us all, not only enjoyment and pleasure and (for many) a lasting love of the theatre, but some sense of the glory of language, the music of words, the role of image and symbol. Sometimes a well-known acting group were playing in the city. I remember one magic afternoon when the great Anew McMaster brought his players to the college to perform for us. It must have been 1943. They did scenes from *Macbeth, Othello, The Merchant of Venice, Little Lord Fauntleroy*. All the Fathers from the community were invited over to the auditorium – they would at that time have been forbidden by Canon Law to attend a public performance!

The big Easter experience each year was the opera, always Gilbert and Sullivan. If any of the many schools and centres in Limerick city produced other light operas, *Maritana* or *The*

Bohemian Girl, we went to see them too. We studied Grand Opera a little. Gounod's *Faust* was to be performed in the city. Fr Jack spent weeks going over the words and score with us. When the curtain went up on the night we knew every note and line. I have never since enjoyed a musical entertainment comparable to that evening.

About twice a week we had gramophone lessons in which we were taught about the great composers. Given that I had a very slim talent in music, it was no poor start in life to leave the college, as I did, with a love of Beethoven, Haydn, Chopin and Brahms, as well as a great love for the music of song, especially the songs of Franz Schubert.

But there was more to come. Fr Jack Treacy had collected a miniature gallery of paintings and masterpieces in the study hall. The gallery was later to spread down the stairs and along corridors. Two or three nights a week we got short talks on the world's paintings. We learned to distinguish the various 'schools', the Florentine, the Venetian, the English, the French. We learned to distinguish the Dutch masters from the German. We learned about impressionism and post-impressionism and cubism. When I left I could make a fair shot at recognising a Rembrandt or a Vermeer or a Manet or a Constable. Once, as a young priest, I rather startled a parish priest by commenting on a piece of valuable sculpture which he prized. I said it reminded me of Rodin's famous statue of Balzac. He looked at me sharply: 'Where did you go to school?' he asked.

* * *

One is always more favourably disposed towards the teachers of one's favourite subjects. Mine were History and English. We studied the classics, Latin and Greek, and successfully, I must add, mainly due to the robust methods of Fr Willie

Murphy. I will pass over Mathematics with the tribute of my silence; it was all I could ever offer before its mysteries. I used to blame the teacher for my failure in even the simplest tasks of adding and subtracting. He was, I believe, a very bad teacher but I realise now that he got a very poor start with me.

Our History lecturer was Fr Paddy O'Donnell. He loved the subject himself and it showed. The past came to life and you were caught. He would read to us, when studying the Tudor period, for example, from books like *Catherine of Aragon* by Garret Mattingly, or *Characters of the Reformation* by Hilaire Belloc. I remember History suddenly coming alive one morning as he read from *The Great O'Neill* by Seán Ó Faoláin. I don't put much store by examination results but during my time in his class one student in the Intermediate Certificate exam got first in Ireland.

Fr Michael Minihan taught English and he gave a great love of his subject to his students. His teaching was quite unique. It combined the imparting of information with a great freedom of spirit and what is vital: a great encouragement of individual gifts and potential. Once when he was being enthusiastic about some poem, somebody in the class said, 'Father is that poem on the Leaving Course?' 'What does it matter?' he replied, 'Don't you see it's beautiful?' We did.

Those were the years of the Second World War when the powerful speeches of Winston Churchill were part of people's conversation. One morning Michael Minihan came into class. It was shortly after the defeat of the Germans led by the great Field Marshall Rommel, at El Alamein in North Africa. He read the opening lines of Churchill's latest speech: 'Three Sundays ago we rang the bells for Alamein.' Then he stopped. 'You see', he said, 'he did not say, "the battle of Alamein" or "El Alamein". Just the simple word "Alamein". Far more powerful.' It was a great way to learn the English language.

The results showed. Somewhere around 1942 there was a

national essay competition promoting the cause of the canonisation of Oliver Plunkett. Thousands of students entered from all over the country. We were a tiny school of sixty but we won five prizes and the first and third place in Ireland.

* * *

But a picture is a picture and the shadows are part of the light. The Redemptorist Secondary School in Limerick was extremely strict. So much so that many who went through over those years, many now Redemptorists, would look back on it, if not in an embittered way, certainly very adversely. Only those who had some idea of going on to join the Congregation were allowed to come or to stay. Discipline was, by our standards now, quite extraordinary. There was reading at table, there could be no talking in twos, no exclusive friendships, no hands in pockets, no eating between meals, no mixing whatever with outsiders, no competitive games with other schools, no newspapers, no pocket money carried around, no letters received unless first inspected by the Director.

We were not supervised at study in the Study Hall or during examinations – a code of honour reigned which, I'm sure, in many a young heart was a code of fear. Discipline was controlled by prefects known as 'Angel Guardians' (there were eight of them), with a head prefect known as the Capo. Any violation of rule or regulation observed by the guardians resulted in the guilty one being 'sent up'. This meant that after night prayers you had to go to the Director's room and report your offence. It was not always the ordeal it may sound but it did sometimes result in severe punishment, though never physical punishment like caning.

But, of course, humanity kept breaking in. 'Angel Guardians' would warn you, 'let you off', be easy and understanding. One I remember particularly never sent anyone up. These were early signs I'm sure of a decency and sensitivity and depth of heart which later flowered into good, even excellent priests or laymen!

And Fr Jack Treacy himself was not untouched by humanity. That was his strength. He was gruff, dismissive, intimidating, schoolmasterish in a very demanding way, but he had a soft streak, he was humane and, incidentally, a very good confessor. While he did not get the balance right (as many would claim) his heart was right. All told, he was the source of a great deal more good than harm.

One small personal reproach I have always held against Fr Jack. Being from a hurling county (Tipperary) I loved the game but Fr Jack Treacy forbade it. Where his antipathy came from I do not know, but for him a young fellow with a hurley in his hand was not just dangerous, he was a killer! There was talk for a while of his allowing hurling with 'a five-yard rule'. That is, apparently, you could not go within five yards of anyone, especially when he had the ball! I never saw this version of the game played but I did meet a priest who had gone through the college before me. His comment was: 'One just felt silly playing "five-yard-rule hurling", to say nothing of the feelings of those watching it.'

One final thing must be said: boys entered the Redemptorist College when they were about twelve or thirteen. They would, in the normal course of events, be eighteen or nineteen on completing the Leaving Exam. These are very sensitive and fragile years for boys coming to terms with awakening sexuality. They need a lot of help and understanding. I believe we got this from the Redemptorists. Our confessors were all Redemptorists and they were excellent. We saw nothing of the blood and heard nothing of the thunder which, to a quite unreasonable extent, now surrounds the memory of many who attended Redemptorist parish missions and retreats. But there was, all the same, an over-emphasis on purity and the dangers of sex, to the point that the experience left a deep scar of scrupulosity and nervousness which, for some of us at least, took a long, long time to heal

🐞 🐞 🐞

I cannot claim it now but there was a time when I could recite hundreds of lines of Chesterton's great poem *The Ballad of the White Horse*. With its atmosphere of chivalry, of open air and open seas, of battles lost and won, of high hopes and gloom, of loyalty and despair, of faith and friendship, it stands supremely in my mind for Cluain Mhuire, the beautiful major seminary, overlooking Galway Bay, in which I spent my eight years in preparation for ordination and life as a missionary.

> *O go you onward; where you are*
> *Shall honour and laughter be,*
> *Past purpled forest and pearled foam,*
> *God's winged pavilion free to roam,*
> *Your face that is a wandering home,*
> *A flying home for me.*

After taking our first vows, following a year of novitiate in Dundalk, we went on to begin studies in the major seminary. Cluain Mhuire was then, in 1945, just a few years old, and was to last only fifty years. It is now closed and sold.

The course of studies began with three years at University College Galway, mostly for an arts degree. Those who did not attend university attended Rhetoric, a two-year course in the humanities. This was what I did. I was later to study for an education degree in the Dominican University of Santo Tomas in Manila.

Next came two years of Philosophy and concurrently subjects like Church History and Elocution. Then followed two years of Dogmatic Theology and Scripture. In the last two years we studied Moral Theology. It helps one to learn about right and wrong, what one can do and what not. With their pastoral approach to preaching the Gospel, with the immediate demands for answers in the confessional and the consulting room, with their experience of people as they live out life in all its confusions and doubts, Redemptorists have always set great store by an expertise in moral theology. This goes back to their founder, the great moral theologian and patron of confessors, Alphonsus de Liguori.

* * *

If I were to compare the two educational approaches in my time, that of our minor seminary in Limerick and that of the major seminary, Cluain Mhuire would come off badly. In Cluain Mhuire we went through the prescribed ecclesiastical subjects but the limitations of the 'going through' left a lot of leeway. In the 1950s and 1960s we were in the last days of the manual or textbook approach. This approach was not education in any real sense.

Our textbook, for example in Dogmatic Theology or Moral Theology, was really an enlarged, detailed and sometimes sophisticated catechism. It was, at the end of the day, questions and answers. You learned the answers. In the hands of a very good teacher with an open, imaginative and venturesome approach the textbook was fine but we did not, generally speaking, have that kind of teacher. I can still hear the professor in one branch of theology announce the material for the next class with the words 'Gentlemen, for the next day, pages 241 to

247'. Not the remotest hint of preparation, clarification (what was important and what was not) or reminder.

The weakness of this bondage to the textbook became very clear if a student wanted to do some general reading himself. You had to get permission for every book borrowed from the library. That in itself was wise and not a great burden. But the problem was this: nearly all extra reading in literature, theology, history, whatever, was looked upon by the teaching staff with suspicion. Were you studying the textbook? Were you preparing for class with its questions and answers? One particular teacher – on my going to him with a certain book – sent me from pillar to post around the staff to clear the book. It might, he said, contain something forbidden by the Church. The book, incidentally, was *City without Walls: An Anthology of Religious Writing* edited by Margaret Cushing Osgood. The real reason, of course, for this near-charade was that I might, by general reading, be neglecting my studies!

Let me illustrate by contrast. We had one excellent teacher in Cluain Mhuire: Fr Seán Ó Ríordán. He stood out. I am quite sure he could have lectured in any of the major subjects (or minor ones) but my class, luckily, had him for Bible Studies. We had a textbook in Scripture written by three Spanish Redemptorists (Simon, Prado and Durado) in impenetrable Latin but Fr Seán never referred to them. He had a most engaging, lively approach to lecturing. He opened vistas, he encouraged, he loved questions. If education has anything to do with leading the human spirit up on to the broad sunlit uplands he was an educator. I recall one class (I believe we were studying the Psalms) in which Fr Seán never mentioned the Bible. He gave us a picture of the Middle East, he told us about the role of oil there, he fixed in our minds the endless sands, the nomadic life, the sun's anvil – out of all of which the Revelation came. You cannot begin to understand the Bible in a better way.

If being a good teacher has anything to do with enthusing young minds (and it has) then Seán Ó Ríordán was a good teacher. There are books still unread by me which I bear in mind to read because of his enthusiasm so long ago. One cannot offer one's teacher a greater word than that; and it gives me particular pleasure to do so.

But, as always, the picture has to be completed. For the greater number who went through with me, there were marvellous times in Cluain Mhuire. We put on two formal plays every year, one in English and one in Irish. Those of us who love acting and the stage recall our experiences with the greatest pleasure, not forgetting the topical 'Reviews' (know as 'stunts'). For those interested in music there was a student orchestra, a very good radio and gramophone system, concerts and lectures. We started, in my time, a Literary, Historical and Debating Society.

And, of course, many of us read widely – in spite of restrictions! This was particularly true of the summer holidays. As we did not go home to spend summer with our families, we had a holiday house in Clifden. For five weeks each year we students had a dream time: reading, swimming, rowing, climbing, walking. The odd visit now to Connemara and its mountainous beauty leaves me a little lost and with a deep longing for those marvellous summer weeks in the West.

> *In the slopes away to the western bays,*
> *Where blows not ever a tree,*
> *He washed his soul in the west wind*
> *And his body in the Sea.*

* * *

For six of the eight years of my time in Cluain Mhuire (and for the whole year of my novitiate preceding it) our superior was Fr John McDonnell. In appearance he was cold and a little forbidding, in reality he was both. But the vast majority of students admired him. He was deeply devoted to the ideals of the Redemptorist Congregation, even to the details of its traditions and living. Yet he was kindly in his ·person-to-person relations with students. He was a very good listener and a very good respecter of one's individual spirituality. He was also quite broad-minded. Towards the end of my time as a student I asked him if I could get permission from him for all books as I was having trouble with teachers in the other disciplines. He said yes. He had one matchless quality when it came to dealing with young people: he was immensely fair and just. I was alone with him when he died at a fairly young age. The turmoil and changes following Vatican II affected him deeply. He thought he saw the end of many of the things he held dear. Few of us who knew him well would respect his memory any the less for that.

🐺 🐺 🐺

An interest in books and an enthusiasm for reading are largely a matter of temperament. The claim that if young people grow up in a home where there are books or are encouraged when young to read, then they will be readers is not upheld by experience. If you are a reader you are a reader. I have always been one.

I began with the usual children's classics: *Alice in Wonderland, Swiss Family Robinson, Grimm's Fairy Tales, Anderson's Fairy Tales, Gulliver's Travels, Robin Hood.* I moved on to the *Thirty-nine Steps,* the *Mysteries of Edgar Wallace, The Invisible Man* by H. G. Wells, *Ivanhoe, Robbery Under Arms* by Rolf Boldrewood, *The Iron Pirate* by Max Pemberton. As we had reading at table in secondary school those of us with a reading bent were further encouraged. By the time I sat the Leaving Cert I was a confirmed reader. The literature of the young, of itself, with its excitement and action, carries the young reader along: it is the eternal appeal of the story. But once students move into the eighteen- or twenty-year bracket they need guidance. I noticed a recent comment on Malcolm Bradbury's book, *The Modern British Novel.* The reviewer said, 'It is a book which ought to be prescribed reading for sixth-formers studying A-level English and for University students. It supplies what is so often lacking in their studies: the historical context of individual books.'

Without taking sides in the debate over the relationship between an artist's life and that artist's work, I think it is important that the context or the ambience out of which a book has come be pointed out by teachers and understood by readers. In one of the most helpful books for me long ago, (*The World's Ten Greatest Novels*) Somerset Maugham wrote: 'I think that to know what sort of a person the author was adds to one's understanding and appreciation of his or her work. To know something about Flaubert explains a good deal that would otherwise be disturbing in Madame Bovary and to know what little there is to know about Emily Brontë gives a greater poignancy to *Wuthering Heights*, her strange and wonderful book.'

In all my years in Cluain Mhuire we never got a hint of help in this direction. We did have classes in general English but they were unimaginative. It was accepted that students did some reading but apart from the fact that a few ecclesiastical biographies were supposed to be read, there was no other advice. I remember just one tiny piece of help offered me. I mentioned to the lecturer in Church History that I was about to start reading Tolstoy's *War and Peace*. 'A great book', he said, 'but don't read it until you are forty.' It was good advice and I followed it.

What effect all this had on others I don't know but it has left me regretful. It was not too bad when reading English or Anglo-Irish literature. We knew enough about our own country, about Elizabethan history, about the Puritans, about the atmosphere of the Restoration, about the Romantic movement, about the Victorians, to read the literature of those various times with some sense. It was when we came to backgrounds of which we knew little or nothing that the problem became clear.

As a student I became very attracted to French literature, particularly of the nineteenth and twentieth centuries. I read mostly in translation but some in French. Recalling off-hand a few authors makes my point: Honoré de Balzac, Prosper Mérimé, Alexander Dumas, Alphonse Daudet, Anatole France, Victor Hugo, Charles Peguy, François Mauriac, George Bernanos, Paul Claudel, Henri Gheon, René Bazin.

If ever there was a mixed bag of books that was it. If ever the background needed to be explained there it was. Turbulent French movements – religious, social, political, regional – touched all this literature and were the key to its full enjoyment, but I was lost. I am not saying that in our major seminary we should have had experts in European literature. That would be nonsense. I am only using the French example to show that, in general reading, students need help and we did not have it.

Years after the whole experience of Cluain Mhuire was over I received a letter from a lifelong friend. He had been a classmate and an ordained Redemptorist but is now out of the active priesthood and happily married in the United States. He used a phrase over which most of us who had shared those years together would stand. He called them the 'great and happy times in Cluain Mhuire', which they were. Those of us who have revisited the old building as it stands now, sold and gone, have looked in silence and have felt desolate.

I was ordained to the priesthood in Cluain Mhuire on

Sunday, 17 August 1952. There were four of us. Standing beside me that morning was Fr John Bennett from Belfast. We had gone together as boys to the Redemptorist College in Limerick on 22 August, 1938. Next day, twenty others were with us in that Intermediate I class. We two were the only survivors.

🐜 🐜 🐜

On leaving Cluain Mhuire and after the completion of our studies in 1953 we faced one final act of preparation: the Second Novitiate.

This was a little time of spiritual renewal but mostly of sermon writing. It lasted six months. All around us in the universal Church, the Irish Church, the social scene, things were fairly static. There were volumes of set sermons which we each rewrote according to our own needs. An elderly priest in the community gave me a look at the text of his sermon on Confession. He said I could use it, that it was a good one. He had been preaching it since 1913!

I should be very slow to be too adversely critical of all this. When a young Redemptorist, at that time, set out to preach a mission, usually with a more experienced confrére, he had ready a set number of sermons. He had the subject of each clearly in his mind – it was orderly and clear also for his hearers. Without exception we would all have been trained to speak well, project our voices, be distinct. In no branch of our preparation was the discipline as strict as in that of elocution.

Added to this was a very special Redemptorist thing: simplicity. In our training, especially in the Second Novitiate, this was first. We must use language which was acceptable to the most educated of our audience, free from solecism or slang, proper, grammatical and at the same time capable of being understood by the most unlettered. This was one expression of what is now called a charism, handed down from the founder, St Alphonsus. Distinguished theologian and writer though he was, he held in as much zeal and love the one whom he called 'any poor old ignorant woman' as he did a princess of the realm.

One of the most widely-heard phrases used to describe Redemptorist missionaries was 'the hell-fire preachers'. Nor does it seem possible to cast the thing off, even now, in spite of massive evidence to the contrary. All I can say is that between 1953 and 1955 (my first term as a missionary) I saw none of it.

Taking a week's preaching, Sunday to Sunday, I can recall the approach. We began with an opening sermon which was a general look at the challenge of God's Revelation to the world and the world's response. On Monday the sermon dealt with our great failure in response: sin. This sermon lent itself naturally to a dramatic presentation, often in the context of God's punishments and our eternal loss. On Tuesday there was a sermon on the great remedy, confession, the sacrament of reconciliation with God. By Wednesday the positive fight-back had begun. There was that night a sermon on prayer 'the great means of salvation'. Thursday evening saw a moving celebration of the greatest of the prayers, the Holy Mass, and its gift to us of the Abiding Sacrament on the altar. A sermon on the Passion and Death of Christ on Friday served as a repetition and reminder of all that was said during the week. There was a sermon on Saturday on Our Lady, the first and greatest Christian.

The closing sermon on Sunday night varied a great deal. The best one I heard in those years was on Heaven. The night always concluded with a renewal of our baptismal vows. The dramatic use of dialogue here, while effective on the night, often lent itself, in the telling afterwards, to more mimicry and anecdote than were helpful. All told, however, the preaching was positive and truly intended to be sympathetic, helpful and hopeful.

I would have, from my memory, the same to say about mission confessions. There were some intractable problems, not all of them the making of the confessors, especially in the area of sexuality. No doubt individual priests could be harsh and insensitive but the overall idea was that we should be understanding and helpful. I remember the superior coming to me on one mission. A group of travelling people were attending each night and they were coming for confession this particular day. The superior was unable to attend to them so he asked me to hear their confessions. I was sharply instructed to be kind and understanding, to remember their way of life, not to be over-demanding or too insistent on anything. They were good people. The most modern moral theologian would be pleased!

Looking back, in general, I would have to say that Redemptorist missions, as I started on them, did not bear the remotest resemblance to the picture painted of them in Austin Clarke's raw and savage poem, 'The Redemptorist':

> *While proud of the Black Cross on his badge,*
> *The Liguorian at Adam and Eve's*
> *Ascended the pulpit, sulphuring his sleeves*
> *And setting fire to the holy text.*

Even making the widest allowance for poetic licence, as literature the poem is singularly uninformed.

Few people realise that one of the most far-reaching of the revolutions which Vatican II planned was meant to take place in the pulpit. This is not to say that sermons in the past were bad and now they are good. A case can actually be made for saying that sermons in the past were very good (in their time) and sermons today are bad; as many of them are.

Sermons in the 1950s and earlier were what we call 'objective'; they dealt with what was 'fixed', what was 'out there'. We preachers had come from the manual tradition. We were used to questions and answers and repeated them in the pulpit – sometimes very dramatically and very well. We explained the Church's teaching, what you could do and what you could not, when and when not. Condemnation and denunciation came readily in this context. Incidentally, it is not difficult to write and preach a sermon laying about one! And, it has to be said, audiences were not averse to enjoying such sermons, as attested by the extra large attendance when people were expecting the preacher to deal with certain subjects.

But it is the negative side of such preaching which is significant. There was no hint offered that the Faith was more a 'search' than a 'find', that we had more questions than answers on our plate. There was no attempt to teach people about conscience; indeed, listening to some now one would think that conscience was a modern invention. There was very little trust in people and no attempt at all to get them to trust themselves. The famous journalists' dictum was unheard by the preachers: 'Give light and the people will find their own way.'

There was, in fact, little effort made to get people to think, which, when you look at it, is strange for Christians, we who bear the name of the One who was always striving to get people to reflect: 'Look', 'See', 'Behold', 'You have ears, can you not hear?', 'How do you read it yourself?'

Perhaps the most deadening hand laid on preaching in the past was the idea: 'don't say anything which might be too difficult to understand.' We used that phrase 'the ordinary people' – they wouldn't understand. As G. K. Chesterton said: 'Where does one find an ordinary person? I never met one.' Only slowly have preachers heard the liberating call of Cleverly Ford: 'Pitch your preaching up a little.' What choice do we have? Never to lead people on further, never to ask them to cut their teeth, keep saying the usual, obvious things. No wonder our preaching is boring!

The greatest fault in the preaching of the past was theological. We tended to concentrate on sin, mainly, I'm sure, because we wanted to be practical. Is this a sin? Is that a sin? How far can you go? There is now, unfortunately, a swing in the opposite direction and we hear the plea 'don't moralise in your preaching'. We must to some extent. As Chesterton said: 'A teacher who is not being dogmatic is not teaching.'

What we did not have in our preaching in the past, was an awareness of the order of events, as it were. First and foremost God's revelation, the Faith, is a gift. Central to the Bible is – not the Ten Commandments – but the Word, the Good News that God would be our God and we his dearly loved children. Secondly, the Faith is a promise. Its Good News sows in our hearts a high hope for the here and the hereafter. As St Paul put it to the early Christians, the hope that was theirs was 'the lesson which you learned from the life-giving message of the Gospel'. We cannot stand before a gift offered, before a marvellous promise made, without some reaction on our part. This is the third step. It is only here that we find ourselves on the familiar ground of sin and virtue, of acting or reacting well or poorly towards God.

Some such approach in the past, more widely put, would have helped to locate sin 'in its place', would certainly have given us a less mechanistic view of the practice of the Faith, would have made us, in fact, a little more mature as the children of God.

The kind of preaching which the Church today should favour (and we often find) is quite different from that of the past. The very approach differs. What is demanded of the preacher, to begin with, is a profound respect for people, for the hearer. We must bear seriously in mind that God's Spirit is at work in human hearts. As Karl Rahner said: 'He is there before we arrive.' Or, as the good old common-sense Englishman Samuel Johnson said: 'People need to be reminded rather than instructed.' It would be enormously helpful if we bore this in mind in an area like sexuality. In fact, it is the teaching of the Church. A recent declaration from Rome stated: 'the more the faithful appreciate the value of chastity the better they will understand, *by a kind of spiritual instinct*, its moral requirements and counsels.'

Following naturally on a respect for people, the preacher must have a trust in them. By encouraging people to be thoughtful, prayerful, reflective, we will help them hear the Voice of the Spirit; they will find their own way. This is particularly helpful when talking to young people. In one of his great statements, the *Pastoral Institution on the Mass Media*, Pope Paul VI said: 'Naturally parents will wish their children to use the media in a proper manner. Nevertheless, let them trust the young because they have been born and have grown up in a different kind of society. Because of this they are better forewarned and better forearmed to meet the pressures that come from every side' (*Communio et Progressio*).

Closely allied, in the preacher, to trust in people must be an acceptance of personalism, of the subjective in modern life. One of the most powerful forces in the human heart today is personalism. Influenced, among other things, by the widespread popularisation of the so-called depth sciences (psychology, psychoanalysis etc.) people today regard their feelings as paramount. They regard themselves ('I', 'Me', 'Myself') as paramount. We may not like this and it has far-reaching results but it is a fact. Preachers had better bear it in mind when they try to communicate.

Articulating, putting into words how people feel, growing in the skills of communicating how the preacher himself feels, is the highway to success in today's pulpit. But the articulation of how people feel is not done for its own sake: we are preaching a message. The very point of being aware of people's feelings is that we might throw the light of God's love and care across the areas of life where most people today feel at home.

And none of this is easy, even though it may seem so. We have all sat through attempts which have quickly degenerated into pub-talk and the fatuities of the worst television. The kind of preaching called for today actually needs a great deal of thought and preparation. Any notion that a preacher can begin with the chatty line, 'As I was sitting in the sacristy, jotting down a few notes, it just struck me…' and take it from there, is a big mistake. We have all seen and heard it made.

Finally, there is the little (and great) matter of mystery. There is no sense in trying to communicate the Christian message, the Revelation of God, without an acceptance on the part of people of the idea of mystery. In our materialistic and scientific world this may, in the end, be the greatest obstacle to the successful preaching of the gospel. We must move it.

There is a story told in the life of the famous German philosopher and missionary Albert Schweitzer. He spent the First World War interned as an alien in France but he knew what was going on. He claimed that the young men who went through the terrible experiences of the Western trenches were of two kinds. One group went trained in the tradition that the Faith had all the answers, that we know what God is like, that things are black and white, but they came back from the trauma of Flanders without a shred of faith in anything. The other group were trained in the schools which taught that life is a mystery, that there are more questions than answers, that God is the greatest of the mysteries, that hope in the end is all we have. They came back with their faith intact. I believe it.

In 1955, having worked for two years on missions and retreats in this fascinating world of preaching and learning to communicate, it all suddenly stopped. It was a Saturday morning early in Lent. I was about to leave Limerick, with two others, on a mission to a parish in Waterford city. I received a message from the Reception. The provincial superior wanted to see me for a moment before I left. I made my way to his office. After greeting me he shuffled some papers on his desk and said, 'Ah yes, here it is. Your boat will be sailing from Southampton, for the Philippines, on Sunday, July 24th. It is a good line, North German Lloyd. Keep it to yourself for the moment. By the way, give my kindest regards to the parish priest in Waterford, Dean Kelleher. All success to the mission.'

🐜 🐜 🐜

In the age of sail, the Spanish galleon, for all her majesty, was a bad proposition in the water. She moved very slowly, took a great deal of punishment from wind and sea and was a prey to hostile men-o'-war. Medicine was still primitive. Means of keeping food and water unspoilt hardly existed. Long sea voyages, consequently, took a dreadful toll on the health and even on the lives of travellers. The journey from Spain to the Philippines – through Mexico – combined the two longest sea journeys of all. With time allowed for recuperation in Mexico after the Atlantic crossing, the trip took close to two years. (*Small Net in a Big Sea*, Michael Baily).

If anything, that description of missionaries travelling to Asia is benign. Certainly those who went from Europe the other way (going East) have put a far more harrowing account on paper, as illustrated in '*Jesuits Go East*' by Felix Alfred Platner. It is an unbelievable tale of endurance, illness, thirst and death.

But that was 250 years ago and more. When we stepped aboard our ship off Southampton in 1955 bound for the East, we walked on to a first-class hotel. It was the *Hessenstein*, sailing out of Hamburg. The Second World War had ended only ten years before. Some reminders of that terrible time were still in place. The Germans, for example, could not come in to Southampton – we had to board the *Hessenstein* from a tender on the high seas.

But they were leaving their troubles swiftly behind them. In 1945 Germany was, literally, a heap of rubble. The city of Hamburg, from which our ship had come, was so heavily bombed in one winter that the fires lasted for ten or twelve days on end. So great was the heat that in one month of January the leaves and blossoms in the neighbouring forest started to bloom. Yet here were the Germans back in business, with a fleet of cargo-passenger ships plying the oceans. Our ship, the *Hessenstein*, had in its hold something like fifty Volkswagens bound for Ceylon, now Sri Lanka. I can't say that our ship's company won our affection but as Germans they certainly won our admiration.

It took five weeks to reach Manila. Three of us were travelling abroad for the very first time. To really enjoy such a journey of 13,000 miles one needs not only an interest in geography but a feel for history as well. Names and their echoes kept coming into hearing and sight: Cape St Vincent, Gibraltar, Corsica, Elba, Pantellaria, Malta, Ismailia, Sinai, the Red Sea, Cape Comorin, the most southerly point of India, Singapore. One sharp memory has stayed with me from that journey, that of thirst. Fresh Irish blood was meeting tropical heat for the first time. No amount of the beautiful German beer could ease the craving.

There was an excellent library on the *Hessenstein*, including the complete works of a number of English writers. I recall reading *The Summing Up* by Somerset Maugham and, very specially, his moving novel *Of Human Bondage*, perhaps the greatest monument to loneliness in the language. If ever reading can be said to come into its own it is on a long voyage at sea.

I went to the Philippines twice by boat but enjoyed the second time more than the first, due mainly, perhaps, to the widespread use of English aboard as well as to other cultural factors. This time the boat was the *Patroclus* of the British Blue Funnel line. We sailed out of the Mersey in early February 1962, with the added bonus of some very interesting port calls on the way.

One day, while en route in Rotterdam, a group of us organised a tour of Holland. We went to Amsterdam to visit the Rijksmuseum with its great Rembrandt masterpiece, *The Night Watch*. We visited the Hague and the Peace Palace. We went on to Delft and saw the original scenes of many of Vermeer's paintings. We saw part of the Atlantic Wall built by Hitler to guard Festung Europa. We saw the headquarters of Seyss-Inquart, the Nazi who was Military Governor of Holland in the war years. Arthur Seyss-Inquart was an Austrian Catholic who left no happy memories among Hollanders. He had a limp, they told us, and his name has gone into the Dutch language to describe a similar affliction. Symbolic in a way of the whole Nazi experience: it was a deep, crippling wound inflicted on Europe; and the scars remain.

At the deepest layer of Christian consciousness, of Christianity itself, there are two or three things which have shaped its destiny. One of them is the call to the foreign missions. The Church was at one and the same time founded and sent: 'Full authority in heaven and on earth has been committed to me. Go forth therefore and make all nations my disciples. And be assured I am with you always to the end of time.' The theology of Vatican II stressed that each local Church is the Universal Church in that particular place, and so, built into the idea of my native parish is the obligation and the challenge to have an eye for the whole earth.

One of the most striking illustrations of this can be found in the countless broken pieces of Christianity found across the world. They may, separately, be heretical, schismatic, misguided or wrong, but they are on their way, their missionaries out, spreading the News as they see it.

In our time the foreign missionary ideal has run into difficulties. Some of them are of the Church's own making but some are a blessing: they force us to do some serious thinking on what the foreign missions are supposed to be about and what the central message of the Faith actually is. Very positive ideas on people's civilisation, culture and history now dictate the way we approach them. The very methods we use in preaching the Faith, indeed the very forms or expressions of the Faith we would or should see grow 'in foreign fields', have to be looked at and worked at. It is not easy.

But this has to be said: nothing has enriched the Church more than her experience of Foreign Missions. Old ideas have been proved sound or found wanting in new and strange places; new ideas, with a youthful and adventurous touch, have come back to revitalise and renew the old guard.

The explorer Tim Severin has a lovely story about the leader of the First Crusade, Godfrey of Bouillon. When he was dying, far from home, he gave a small box to one of his knights. 'Take it to Europe, to the Chateau Bouillon, he said, 'and then open it.' Obeying his orders the soldier, on his return, opened the box on the battlements of the castle. Immediately the countless tiny seeds inside blew away, landing on walls, in crevices, across fields. Now every June these seeds spring up into life: they bloom as small, delicate pink flowers, a reminder of their kindred far away in Jerusalem. The story itself is a reminder of all the treasures, delicate, small and great which have been exchanged between the ends of the earth as the Church followed the call: 'Going therefore teach all nations.'

Nor can we accept the dismissive approach to foreign missions which one often hears now: let people alone. They have their own civilisation, culture, history, beliefs. What right has Christianity to go tramping in telling people what to do and what to believe? Put that way, the Church never had the right to do any such thing. But it is on the very point of *right* that the Church makes its stand. If Christianity is true, then people, peoples everywhere, have a right to know about it, have a right to be told, whatever about accepting the News. If this story of Jesus, 'this most tremendous tale of all', is in any way true, then people should be told. The bitterest of all reproaches in human exchange must not, cannot, be laid against Christianity: you never told us!

🐾 🐾 🐾

The Redemptorist link with the Philippines is as old almost as the century. As early as 1902 a Filipino archbishop, preparing for his ordination in Sant' Alfonso in Rome, began negotiations to secure the help of American Redemptorists. This first approach was not successful, but within three years the Irish Redemptorist Provincial had arrived in the Philippines (December 1905). Three months later, fittingly on St Patrick's Day, he took possession of our first house in Opon on Mactan. Three months later again seven Irish Redemptorists arrived. Among them was one man whom many from my student days will remember in his old age. He was a shining example of all that was best in the mission tradition: Fr Tom Cassin.

It must be pointed out that the Philippine mission was not a Foreign mission venture in the strict sense, in the sense that the Good News was being brought there for the very first time. Filipinos are very proud of one title, though it carries its own sadness: they are the only Christian nation in the East. What had happened was that the Spaniards had sown the Faith there long ago but, in the revolt against Spain, the country lost most of its priests and religious, they being Spaniards. It was a special kind of crisis. For example, when the Redemptorists arrived in Cebu the local bishop had sixty vacant parishes in a diocese of two million people. He really needed help.

Arising from this you get the very strong emotional tie which exists between Irish Redemptorists and that far-off land in the South China Sea. Some time in the mid-1940s there was talk of the Irish leaving the Philippines and concentrating on their missions in India and Sri Lanka. There was, not surprisingly, uproar. In few other places outside southern Italy in the days of the founder did his followers find such ideal, typical, Redemptorist country: Catholics, unlettered, without the sacraments, uninstructed but believing, welcoming and eager. We had come, as never before, on those who were in the mind of Alphonsus 'the most abandoned souls'. He would have founded his Congregation again for this.

I spent over fourteen years in the Philippines and any account I should give of my time there would have to begin on that very point of emotion. Twenty-five years after I left the East I was in Brazil, representing Ireland at the World Congress of the International Catholic Union of the Press. The Redemptorist rector in Fortaleza, Fr Phil Hearty, kindly asked me to say a few words to the people at Mass (he would translate into Portuguese). I readily agreed. It happened to be the five-hundredth anniversary to the day when Columbus waded ashore at Hispañola in the Caribbean in 1492. The Faith had arrived in the Americas from Spain and Portugal, and it had come there in the very same way as it had gone East to the Philippines just a little later and through the very same hands. I thought I would say something about the Philippines and how I was reminded of the link as I stood there. The moment I began to speak I got a total block. I could not say a word. I had to sit down. My time in the Philippines had been a marvellous experience but a most deeply felt one. I thought I had come to terms with it; that evening in Brazil I knew I never would.

Of my fourteen years in the Philippines eleven were spent in what is called 'formation'. Formation is the technical word (in Church language) to describe the years of study and reflection which young people go through in preparation for life as a priest or religious. Those who help them and teach them are included in the term.

The history of formation in the Irish vice-province of Cebu is not a happy one. Perhaps 'happy' is not the right word. It was certainly a zig-zag story. Sometime in the 1930s a young Filipino had become a Redemptorist student but he decided against it after three years. The idea then set in that our way of life did not suit Filipinos. Following the Second World War a second start was made: a kind of minor seminary, St Clement's College in Iloilo. It reduced only a small number of vocations. It is now closed. Then a major seminary was started in Cebu in 1961. This seminary was itself dispersed after about six years and the students were all sent to study in Ireland. The place had actually been started with the help of Irish students. Next, a second minor seminary was started in Cebu and it, too, had only a few years of life. And so it went on.

It would be unfair, of course, to blame anyone specifically for all this but I have no doubt that a great part of the problem was interference from authorities at home. I should not want to comment on anything which happened after I left and it is a great pleasure now to meet, from time to time, young Filipino priests and brothers who have come along since. The Lord was writing straight with the crooked lines.

🐾 🐾 🐾

The Philippines is an island group in the Pacific. One has to be careful about the word 'islands'. It is not part of the official title of the modern Republic and it carries certain colonial undertones. Sometimes on our TV news one hears a reference to the island of Mindanao, implying some rather smallish place. Mindanao is far larger than Ireland! The Filipinos first arrived in their islands in great waves of migration, from Borneo mainly, as their literary epics show. They pushed the Negrito aborigines into the mountains and so made the archipelago Malayan. The nearness of a mighty race like the Chinese had a far-reaching influence. A large proportion of present-day Filipinos have Chinese blood in their veins. Under the general umbrella of Malayan, the Filipinos are racially many. For example, Tagalogs, Visayans, Bicols, Ilocanos. These ethnic groups are closely allied to the ethnic groups in Borneo from which they came.

Foreigners have a problem with the many languages and dialects of the Filipinos. They belong to the Malayo-Polynesian family of tongues, as indeed do one-eighth of all the languages of the world.

In contradiction of Kipling's famous line about East and West and 'ne'er the twain shall meet', they actually meet in the Philippines. Two accidents of history brought this about. The first was the 'discovery' of the Philippines by the great explorer Majellan in 1521. The second was when Commodore Dewey sailed his Americans into Manila Bay in 1898. The coming of Spain brought Christianity and what was left of a Graeco-Roman civilisation; the coming of the Americans brought democracy and the English language.

As with all colonial ventures the blessings in practice were mixed. The Spanish Conquest brought the Faith and nationhood. The Filipino people would not have been a nation but a conglomeration of tribes were it not for the Spanish Conquest. But Spain also imposed a harsh colonial yoke which Filipinos tried to shake off more than once. They did so finally with the revolt of 1896 and the establishment of the first Philippine Republic two years later.

The American conquest, on the other hand, brought greater freedom, economic progress, greater social mobility, better hygiene and democracy and a special regard for 'the common man'. But the US also brought the tawdry literature of the magazine stands, the mores of Hollywood, the plague of advertising, some of the worst expressions of the Coca-Cola culture and a type of mass education which, strangely, has made genuine culture the possession of a very few.

It was against this background that I was appointed to teach English and Latin to secondary school students in 1956.

My happiest times in the Philippines were the six years in St Clement's College in Iloilo. The Director was Fr John Lawlor. If you went to him with your ideas and had thought them through he gave you a free hand, as he did to me and others. Remembering my time as a boy in St Clement's in Limerick and carrying its influences, we improved on what was already a very good school. The education system in the country was not at all like our centralised approach, often with sad results: the standards were very uneven, sometimes very low.

The textbooks in English which I found there were American and excellent – one for each of the four years of secondary level. We started a drama group and put on a play each year. Mindful of one of Fr Jack Treacy's pet projects, I gave, throughout the school year, illustrated talks on the great masters of painting and sculpture. John Lawlor, a music enthusiast, did the same for good music. I introduced a reading programme. Before I did so I had to take one amusing step. We had to ban comics. The comic strip, with its colour and movement, has a great appeal for Filipinos. One of my first surprises, when I arrived, was to see a grown man avidly reading a comic book on an inter-island steamer. Our problem with the comics was twofold: the dialogue, both in spelling and structure, was appalling and, worse, the story-line was usually taken from the great stories of both English and American literature – thereby destroying the initial attraction for and interest in good books: the story.

Each student, corresponding to his year, had a set number of books to read. This was linked to the examinations or, as they were always called, 'the tests'. The system had no one final exam with all its cramming, hype and nonsense. Tests took place about every six weeks. Students got used to them and learned from them. Progress could be monitored. The first test was as important as the last.

But – and it is a very large 'but' – these students were

Filipinos, they were Oriental. Were we serving them in full
fairness by producing graduates versed in Shakespeare,
Wordsworth, Keats, Washington Irving, reflecting no
difference from students educated in Ireland or England or
New England? The problem is dramatically expressed by one
of the best educationalists of my time in the Philippines,
Miguel Bernard SJ. He wrote: 'The Filipino is both Oriental
and Occidental and in this dual citizenship lie both his destiny
and his conflict. To be at home in both worlds is his peculiar
perfection; to be confronted with both worlds is his peculiar
burden. His greatest danger is that he might eventually belong
to neither. The Filipino may become an effective bridge
between East and West or he may become an outcast of both
East and West. And since literature is the product of a culture
and the expression of a cast of mind it is by coming to terms
with both horns of this dilemma that Philippine literature will
become great, in whatever language it may be written'
(*Philippine Literature: a Twofold Renaissance*)

To deal in part with this problem I introduced a course in
Philippine Literature in English. It was at least one way of
putting young Filipinos in touch with their own culture, their
own soul, their own self-awareness. At that time, the 1950s,
this literature was just about sixty years old. The English
language had only come with the Americans, but in had come
in force. One of the first groups of US personnel to arrive in
Manila consisted solely of teachers, nearly a thousand of them.
In no time English was being written extensively. In 1928, only
three decades after the introduction of English, an anthology
of short stories was published, edited by José Garcia Villa, now
an internationally recognised poet. But the fascinating fact
about the twenty-four stories in that volume is that they were
selected out of about six hundred stories written in a twelve-
month period from January to December 1928!

Philippine literature in English was naturally, very

derivative and imitative, especially in the beginning. The models were mostly from the US and other English-speaking areas. In 1951 the distinguished Dame Edith Sitwell edited a volume of American poetry, *The American Genius,* but included five poems by José Garcia Villa under the mistaken impression that he was an American!

Gradually, however, Filipinos began to find their feet in English and began to express themselves as themselves. There was a lot of poetry, there were essays, short stories (a great attraction) and some novels. One beautiful novel, dealing with the Japanese Occupation during World War II, was called *Without Seeing the Dawn* by Stevan Javellana. I would place it in any list of worthwhile war literature.

One area in which Filipinos found their feet in English fairly quickly was humour. Filipinos love the funny or bizarre situation, especially against a local background. Alejandro Roces wrote his humorous stories on the subject of cock fighting, always of immense social interest and attraction in the East.

Offering a list of Filipinos who write or wrote in English would not be of very great interest, perhaps, to Western readers but I have always kept an eye on them and enjoyed them. One of the very earliest, if not the first Filipino to write in English was Carlos P. Romulo, later to become well known internationally. He was Secretary of Foreign Affairs and President of the First General Assembly of the United Nations in San Francisco (1945). Incidentally he was, in stature, a very short man. There is a story told of him, probably apocryphal. Just before giving his key-note address to the United Nations he asked an aide for a copy of the telephone directory. The aide replied that it was a very heavy, large tome and offered to look up any number which the President might need. Romulo replied: 'I don't want to check anything in it, I want to stand on it.'

A final comment on Philippine literature in English might best be left to Miguel Bernard. What that literature needed, he said, was 'the added dimension by which Shakespeare and Dante and all truly great writers have tried to present the depths of the human mystery – the theological dimension. This theological dimension, visible in the literature of India and other Oriental countries, is strangely absent from much Philippine writing'.

I left St Clement's College in May 1961, having been appointed to the major seminary in Cebu. My good times were over.

🐜 🐜 🐜

To love at all is to be vulnerable. Love anything and your heart will certainly be broken. If you want to make sure of keeping it intact, you must give your heart to no one....

Wrap it carefully with hobbies and little luxuries; avoid all entanglements; lock it up in the casket of you selfishness. But in that casket – safe, dark, motionless, airless – your heart will change.

It will not be broken; it will become unbreakable, impenetrable, irredeemable...the only place outside Heaven where you can be perfectly safe from all the dangers and perturbations of love is Hell (C. S. Lewis).

Some time ago I was chatting with an old classmate, now for many years a successful priest in the US. In the course of the conversation he said, 'Kevin, priests are the most disloyal bunch of professionals in the world.' I don't believe that for a moment nor, in fact, does he – we all have dark moods. I mention it because it suddenly sounded so real. Discussion on the life and ministry of priests is often unreal, especially in that most sensitive of areas – celibacy and sexuality. The lecture, the sermon, the discussion, the conversation become removed from daily living. You get the exhortation, the eulogy, the ideal, 'the challenge' that terrible word now thrown about with abandon. It actually means something that we don't want, don't know what to do with or that leads us to think 'the sooner we start on this thing the better!'

I find it fascinating that of the dozen or so novels on the priesthood which I have read over the past number of years, only one I would consider worthwhile. It is actually centred on a sinful priest and yet it is enduring in its message (as its title suggests) of the greatness of the priesthood, its power and glory.

A great deal has been written about celibacy in recent times, none better than that by Pope Paul VI in 1967, who bravely faced the questions actually being asked. Looking back, the basic problem about celibacy is: how can what is essentially a free gift given to some come to be made mandatory for all? Looking forward, how will the Church meet the questions now coming 'from out of the press of our time'? In his superb book of theological reflections Fr Thomas Lane writes:

> With a growing positive appreciation of the human body and of marriage, is the celibacy requirement an anachronism? In an age of much breakdown in marriage, is there need for strong witness to married fidelity by those in Church leadership? Have human prescriptions about requirements for ministry been placed before people's right to the Eucharist? Is the insistence on celibacy a subtle form of Church control and Church

power, in ways that negate rather than promote the Good News? Should the Church modify her discipline in cultures where there is no tradition of celibate values? With the many failures of celibates has celibacy ceased to be an effective sign of the kingdom? These are some of the searching questions that will continue to be asked and asked persistently. (*A Priesthood In Tune*)

In between the past and the future is the priest today, myself for example. I have come to feel strongly that celibacy is indeed a gift not given to all, indeed not to many who would otherwise make excellent priests. I say that while at the same time respecting the Church's present discipline. When I meet a young person who is interested in the priesthood but discover that, however willing, he is going to find celibacy a great burden, I advise him to think again. He may (as have countless men before him) carry his celibacy in faithfulness, but I wonder at the price: scrupulosity, severity, legalism, 'too many crusty bachelors and mean old maids'. What about love given and shown? Celibacy is not worth it if is a witness to nothing but will-power.

For myself, I have more or less always felt that I had this gift of celibacy. Not that it made things any easier! I had and have all the normal attraction for those who used to be called in the distancing phrase, 'the opposite sex'. But then, as the confessor said in the seminary long ago 'If you don't find a pretty girl pretty you should not be here.' I was twenty-nine when I went to the Philippines and I certainly found Filipinas very attractive, as they are. Indeed I fell in love more than once over the years.

This is not something which one can fairly be too forthcoming on. Other people's privacy and rights have to be respected. I should not for a moment, for the sake of being dramatic or lurid, involve others, however implicitly. But it is a fact: priests do fall in love as, I am quite sure, do many already married people. Many a marriage, for example, would be saved or deepened if the husband had faced up to realities early on and talked or thought about what was happening to him and that girl in the office. Instead you get the deceptions, the furtive arrangements, the indecisions, the signs of strain and tension and, so often, help coming too late. Or not coming at all.

One of the very first pieces of advice which I found myself giving to young fellow-priests (and I'm sure to myself) was: don't mislead the girl, don't give her wrong impressions, don't build up expectations and; above all, don't plan (sometimes unaware to oneself) to drop things at the suitable time and give no thought to her emotions, her feelings, her heart. Celibacy has a few very unlovely offshoots and one of them is selfishness.

I have over the years, beginning in the Philippines, prayed a great deal and thought a great deal about the very wonderful people whose relationship with me must be described as loving. I owe them more than I can say. They helped me to understand God as love in a way that the sermons and the books never did. I had experience of appreciation and love growing up, especially from my parents, but parents die and the celibate faces the years alone. It is a grace and a blessing (for all) to have human love come into life. It is painful, risky, upsetting, but I dread to think of the mind or inner places of the priest who lives unloved, unloving, in a desert of the heart. How does he pray? How does he preach? God is love: what does that mean for him? George Bernanos wrote: 'I have never met so many hard men as among the clergy of France.'

One of the helpful ways of approaching a particularly troubling or puzzling time in one's life is to sort out the ingredients. I was sent to Cebu city in the summer of 1961 and remained there till my final return to Ireland in 1968. First of all, I was appointed Prefect of Students, that is, the one in charge of the major seminarians. I had no training for this and, inevitably, carried to the task the best and the worst of what I remembered from my own student days. I thought, at the time, that I had grown for the better since my ordination, but looking back now I know I had not, not much. Our monastery in Cebu had been for many years an extremely busy and complex centre. You had a popular church, a giant weekly novena, countless Masses and confessions, missionaries ever on the move, retreats, hospitals, counselling, schools. Looking at the way training is handled now it would probably be regarded as an ideal place for a major seminary. Back in the years 1961-65 that was not at all clear, resulting in, from various angles, tension, disagreement, discontent and frustration.

At midnight of 10/11October 1962 we celebrated a High Mass, coinciding with the opening of the great Vatican Council in Rome. For those interested in signs: as Mass ended a lightning storm struck the central Philippines with a ferocity nobody could remember before. A symbol, in a way, of what was to come at many levels of the Church's life! Not least at the level of student training.

The students in this new seminary had come from three directions. One group came out from Ireland, one group returned from the major seminary in Bangalore, India (a place for which they retained an extraordinary affection) and the third group were straight from the Novitiate in the Philippines itself. I was not aware at the time, nor am I now, of any great problem in this 'mix', but looking back I realise that I was not too alert to very much. Things were happening (often unconsciously) to people's feelings, if not thoughts. Like an earthquake the Renewal began stirring deep down. It had, in fact, begun long before October 1962. People only became aware of things when they broke surface. I am saddened now to think of how little listening I or any of us did, how little sharing, how little talking. Had we then the forms of involvement, exchange and reaction which later became commonplace in community life, things might have been different.

In my years as Prefect of Students no member of staff or community ever came to me and said, 'You are not doing this right.' Nor, indeed, did I ever ask. If a student said anything I would have thought that he was the problem.

One small difficulty was that in that community at large I had no close personal friend with whom I could talk things out. I was always treated very kindly by both superiors and confrères and liked those with whom I lived, but the lines of communication were not many. I have over the years, incidentally, kept friendly relations with all, students and others, who were with me in Cebu then. With only one exception I have never heard an unkind or wounding remark from anyone who was part of that time.

And yet those years are part of me in a way I wish they were not. On the morning of 12 December 1964 new appointments were posted on the notice-board. A new Prefect of Students was named and that is all (apart from one distant comment from a superior) that I ever knew about what happened. They had been very hard years. I had to go into hospital at least five times and there were signs of strain which could have become serious. When I returned to Ireland a few years later I was diagnosed as suffering from two very bad ulcers, which resulted in my spending six months in the Medical Missionaries of Mary Hospital in Drogheda. Thanks to the expertise of a wonderful staff, especially that of the surgeon, Mr Vincent Sheehan, I came out completely cured. In fact, I found a health which I had never know previously, the great gift of health, 'that most elusive form of happiness.'

🐜 🐜 🐜

There is a very common reaction among people which we used to call 'touchiness': 'He is very touchy' about this or that. The word 'touchy' has now given way to 'defensive': we say someone is very defensive about something. I suspect that at the root of this reaction is insecurity. When we are insecure about our actions or ourselves we tend to react to criticism or comment in certain definite ways.

If you look about, in this difficult time for the Church, at all the work which the Church is doing today, its work of evangelisation, its preaching, its attempts to reach people, to save the Faith, to understand the young, to prepare for the future, you will notice that nobody is actually too sure on how to go about things. They wonder: is this the right thing to do or the right way to do it? There are plenty of counter-suggestions and opposition no matter what one does. The result is that one has to be very careful about what one says, implied or otherwise. Defensiveness is all over the place.

I have been talking about my time in the Philippines. I was asked to do there what might be described as specialised work. Few would spend their time there as I spent mine. Many indeed would hardly recognise the Philippine experience which they knew or know in what I have said. But this in no way implies a criticism or a comment on the great and very different task which was and is the Redemptorist's pride there: missions, preaching, administering the sacraments, saving the

Faith in fact. And, twenty-five years after I left the Philippines, things have so changed that only somebody who, for example, has lived through the Marcos dictatorship or seen the impact of new theological thinking, should dare comment on the situation now. But I know enough and have seen enough to pay tribute to the marvellous work for the Faith which Redemptorists – Filipinos, Irish, Australians and New Zealanders – have done and continue to do in the Pacific. I very personally know that my time in the Philippines was the greatest gift which the Good Lord gave to me as a priest. I am grateful. No other experience has come near it. I cannot imagine a time in the future when I would forget it, or lessen in my love for The Land of the Morning.

🐒 🐒 🐒

When I returned to Ireland in 1968 I had every intention of going back to the Philippines, but it was not to be. Any ideas which I had that I would fit in easily into mission work in Ireland were also rudely shattered. 'Rudely' would be a gentle word. For the years 1965 to 1980 (and beyond) saw one of the most confused, upsetting but interesting periods in modern Church history.

The Vatican Council had finished and the work of implementing it had begun. We were caught in a snowstorm of directives, decrees, instructions, declarations. I can recall four major documents on the renewal of the Sacrament of Penance alone – sadly one of the areas in which the renewal has been rather a failure.

A whole new approach was being set up in our celebration of the Eucharist, our administration of the sacraments, our understanding of the laity, our handling of the media, our living of the religious life, our forms of existence as Church and its relations with other Churches. When I left Ireland in 1955 we missioners were preaching on salvation, hell, prayer, Our Lady, death. On my return I found myself, after a short time, preaching on the meaning or mystery of God, on the role of human beings on éarth, on conscience, on leisure, on the quality of life, on the ache in the heart! Where before we preachers said all we had to say in the pulpit, from on high, now we were sitting in parlours and kitchens listening, discerning, sharing.

And into it all on 25 July 1968 came the news which was to throw the whole pastoral scene out of plumb, here and around the world; the famous encyclical letter, *Humanae vitae*. Whatever has to be said about it, for or against, its repercussions have been immense. It is profoundly sad not only that its great central message has largely been passed by but that it has resulted in such lasting alienation and dissatisfaction among Catholics.

In the early 1970s I remember wishing that we could forget all about it, it took up so much time, space, interest and energy, with a thousand other things awaiting our preaching, understanding, acceptance. I recall meeting a group of young secondary school students during a mission on the south side of Dublin. The subject of *Humanae vitae* came up and I was asked by a young fellow of around seventeen or eighteen why was it that when the Pope set up a commission to examine the whole question of artificial contraception he did not accept its findings. I felt like the financier in Chicago before the Wall Street crash! A bootblack, while polishing his shoes, gave him insider information on the Stock Exchange: it was time, he knew, to get out!

I was appointed to a parish mission team in the west of Ireland in 1968 and spent several happy years with it. The feeling began to grow on me and has lasted: priests, the preaching Church, give altogether too much attention to their own actual preaching and pay little enough care to their hearers. We leave them unhelped, unprepared, untilled to receive the grain. The message of the great parable of the Sower and the Seed is lost.

We throw the seed of the Word on to the hard footpath. It does not pass the surface. We do nothing to encourage people to ask questions, especially of themselves, to think aloud, to doubt, to do some little re-education themselves, to develop some of the imagination (slowly being destroyed by the image world of television) so essential to receiving the message of the Bible. As Chesterton pleaded: 'Must a Christ be crucified in every generation for those who have no imagination?'

We throw the seed of the word on to the rocky ground. It is received willingly enough but, in the words of the parable, the hearer 'has no staying power'. There is, in other words, no real commitment. In our world of adverse criticism of Church and clergy, people, in general, tend to be very uncritical of themselves. Why doesn't the priest preach about this or preach well? Why doesn't the bishop say something about that? But what about ourselves in the pews? It takes two to make anything of a sermon but many prefer the great cop-out of blaming others for the state of things and do little to follow up on what has been preached to them, to ask for more, to ask for explanations, to attend a class or raise a finger that the Good News might flower better in their lives. There is no commitment. And preachers do little to change this: they don't till the soil.

We throw the seed of the word among thistles but 'the false glamour of wealth chokes it'. It is strange that so few priests try to help people understand our consumer world or give any hint of how destructive it can be of real values, with its greed, its triviality, its debasing of sex, its sheer materialism. The faith, the word, goodness are very delicate plants and unless people are helped to understand, to negotiate the culture, the context in which they have to keep the faith alive, we, the priests, are failing them, we are not tilling the soil.

But we, the preachers, do not heed. We go on, Sunday after Sunday, preaching our homily and ignoring the kind of world from which the people before us have come, ignoring what it has already done to them as hearers of the word, forgetting the warning of St Paul about his own people: 'Their unbelieving minds are so blinded by the passing God of this age that the Gospel of the glory of Christ cannot dawn on them and bring them light.'

🐜 🐜 🐜

There is no priest or preacher who does not anguish over the loss of belief on the part of young people. I began to notice it gradually. It is too wide a comment but has been made: we are witnessing among the young a drift from the faith unparalleled since St Patrick, and we have, in talking to them, a very good example of where our emphasis and awareness should be, not so much on our own methods of approach to them (these of course are important) but on the young themselves and on what our world (powerfully supported by consumerism and the mass media) is doing to them.

It can be put negatively: if young people today are led by the peer group, self-isolating in entertainment, mindlessly parroting one another and the junk media ('Why is the Church always talking about sex?', 'Why is the Church against everything?'), following the amorality and sometimes sheer rubbish of the agony aunts, sullen and sour in spirit and deportment, if this is true then you have a soil, in which no faith can grow or stay. The faith is a very different thing. Without for a moment saying that young people are evil (of course they are not) we do have to ponder the general *direction* or *thrust* of the words of St John: 'The light came into the world but men preferred darkness to the light because their deeds were evil.'

Or we can put it positively: if a young person is losing his or her faith, they can help themselves by doing something about this themselves: becoming more unselfish, more self-questioning, more independent of mind, giving a freer rein to their own best instincts, becoming more honest, less subjective. Then things can change. The green shoots of faith begin to appear. The Word of Life, again, has said so: 'If you do the truth, you will know the truth and the truth will set you free.'

But, in the end, nobody owes the young a destiny or a faith. We love them but we cannot force them. If the horrible spectre of a pagan world is what they want to build, or be part of, then it will be so. But it will be their building and let them blame no one else. Like all of us, they have a choice. As Pascal said: 'There is enough light for those who wish to see; there is enough darkness for those who do not.'

🐜 🐜 🐜

For all the adverse criticism to which they have been subjected, the priests and preachers of the post-Conciliar Church of the late 1960s and early 1970s did much more than they have been credited with; certainly more than the huge, slow-moving bulk of the laity. Certainly, they were obliged to do so. But many took risks and, most difficult of all, they took chances. It was a big step to leave the safety of the pulpit and the altar and come down among the people. They should have been there always but that does not take from what they did. A Redemptorist mission in the older style was surely the supreme example of the pulpit fortress at work, but the missioners left that pulpit in more senses than one. Between the years 1968 and 1975 Redemptorists began developing house-meetings and group meetings as part and parcel of their mission plan. There was plenty of formal preaching too and parish missioners had always visited the people in the parish, door by door. During the first week of the New Mission, meetings were held in private houses across the parish. Eighteen, sixteen, twenty would attend and a great deal of preaching the gospel (at least preparation for receiving it) was done. It was done in the form of talking, sharing, questioning, listening.

Two central theories or ideas lay behind this new approach to parish missions. One of those ideas referred back, as it were: the basic concept of Christianity as community. Christians are a family or a community or they are nothing. The teachings of Christianity cannot even be lived if they have not the support of the community at large. One of the early documents published to help us at the time said: 'It is unrealistic to ask an individual to breathe the spirit of Christ and live the values he gave us if the moral air in which people exist is polluted, if public opinion is weak, if economic and workday life is unjust and oppressive, if social and recreational life is manipulated and pagan, if personal life is just not free. There are many places you can throw the seed of the word: on the highway, on the stony ground, in the thicket. We are looking for the good soil; and it is a decent Christian community. This is one of the things the New Mission is about.' And the house-meetings were to be a help towards this.

The second idea or theory behind the new mission looked forward. It concerned a sign of the times which has to be respected. It is part of the future. We call it personalism: the absolutely central place given to the individual person in modern culture. We stress the inviolability of the person, his or her rights, preferences, uniqueness, dreams. The idea, in its strength, came from thinking outside the Church and from traumatic political events in this century but was taken up by the Vatican Council, for example in the Declaration on Religious Freedom.

This stress on the importance of the person has far-reaching results and a couple of questionable ones. It is changing, often for the good, our whole approach to things like authority, obedience, vocation, lifelong commitment but, most fraught of all, it has influenced our observance of the moral law. Its devastations in the world of sexuality, for example, are only now becoming apparent.

However, the idea is there and the Church, in the form of missions and retreats for one, has tried to meet this sign of the times. Each person in a house-meeting had a say, an opinion, a light to offer. We talked, listened, learned. We tried to meet people where they were at, as Pope Paul VI put it 'out of the press of their time'.

I was transferred from parish missions in 1975 and have not had experience of all the developments since, and there have been many. But I am happy that I was there at the start because it was the beginning for me of a great learning process and it has continued.

🐞 🐞 🐞

The great modern Russian, Alexander Solzhenitsyn, wrote: 'One thing is absolutely certain: not everything which enters our ears penetrates our consciousness. Anything too far out of tune with our attitudes is lost, either in the ears themselves or somewhere beyond, but it is lost.'

This is one of the central lessons which I only began to learn when working with the modern parish mission and talking to people. I continue to learn about the importance of attitudes, both in others and in myself. We know what an attitude is without, perhaps, being able to describe it. It is, simply, our mental stance, it's our position of mind or heart *vis-à-vis* communication from another. We acknowledge it in everyday life. A teacher will say, 'I can't get through to her, she has a very ugly attitude.' Or a boss will say of a young trainee, 'He is doing well, he is learning, he has a right attitude.' We might describe a right attitude as the pipeline of communication being open. When it is blocked you get the wrong attitude. Things don't get through.

Attitudes are vital in all forms of communication. Examples help best, though in giving them one may appear to be indulging in clichés. But then there is nothing wrong with a cliché. It is very often a truth just a little overworked.

The first attitude which almost naturally comes to mind is that of openness of mind and heart. This does not mean a willingness to accept anything proposed or propounded or to agree with everything or to challenge nothing. As Chesterton said: the function of the open mind is the same as the function of the open mouth and that is to close reasonably soon on something solid!

An attitude of openness means stepping aside from what one has always held or accepted or defended and taking a good look at what is being suggested or claimed, and doing it with some sympathy, thoughtfulness, especially patience.

Irish people are traditionally very conservative, which carries with it many attitudes of the closed mind. Something which one can see demonstrated in an ongoing study like

Prejudice and Tolerance in Ireland by Mícheál Mac Gréil SJ. People who have been trained in a very rigid and fixed form of education have always to be on the watch – priests and religious, for example, certainly up to the recent past. Scripture scholars point out that in the opposition encountered by the demands of Jesus, the Gospels record little rejection of him by sinners but much rejection by those whom he challenged in their religious outlook: the people of the fixed view. St Alphonsus said that the hardest people in the world to convert are priests!

In talking to people about their faith, in trying to adjust them and ourselves to the many changes of emphasis and direction involved in all the 'changes' in the modern Church, we need one attitude above all others. Nothing from the earliest days of the house-meetings was clearer to me than this. I call it the attitude of broad-mindedness. I don't use the word in the popular sense of general tolerance. I use it in the sense of not wanting or allowing oneself to get bogged down in a detail or a mystery or a novelty. Here you have the great modern movement begun at the Vatican Council with its return to the Scriptures and the Fathers and the genius of the Founders and its going forward to the future in reading the signs of the times – and all of it missed or ignored by somebody getting bogged down or making a song and dance about a detail or a rubric or a tradition: altar girls, the family Rosary, clerical dress. More than one house-meeting was destroyed in its purposes by this distortion. But it goes on all the time at different levels. In a recent new edition of the famous *Pears*

Encyclopedia, under the entry 'Roman Catholic Church', you get two sentences: 'The largest Christian denomination. It opposes contraception and the ordination of women'! Two thousand years of extraordinary history reduced to this.

It is not easy to develop in people an attitude of the broad sweep but, until we do, a great deal of updating, a great deal of preaching go amiss. The famous Mahatma Gandhi rejected the 'untouchable' idea in the Hinduism he cherished but that did not prevent him from concentrating on its broad central idea of love. Let us, Christians, learn.

❧ ❧ ❧

There is another attitude strangely missing in Christians, considering where they have come from: the attitude of thoughtfulness. To be fair, there may not have been much call for it by any of us in the last few hundred years. The way authority was exercised, the way religion was taught, even the way morality was practised, all led to a certain acceptance, to a lack of reflection or even a recognition of the need for it.

But Jesus was a thinking man. He grew in wisdom by giving thought to the flowers, the birds, the animal world, the crops. He kept asking his followers to reflect. He encouraged thought by questions: Now who was the man who was neighbour to the one who fell among robbers? Who do you say that I am?

The very first word of his preaching was *Repent*. 'Repent and believe the Gospel. The word repent is the famous *metanoia*, its root meaning to gain insight, to think. Pope Paul VI gave a classic definition of it: 'We can only approach the Kingdom of Christ by *metanoia*. This is a profound change of the whole person by which one begins to consider, judge and arrange one's life according to the holiness and love of God made manifest in his Son in the last days and given to us in abundance' (*Apostolic Constitution Paenitemini*).

We cannot even pray as we should without being thoughtful, reflective. This is the basic idea behind the centuries-old tradition of meditation and contemplation. Without thoughtfulness, prayer becomes very thin gruel indeed. There is a vital lesson in a response of the saintly Archbishop Michael Ramsey. He was asked how long he spent in prayer each day. He replied: 'One minute, but then it takes me half an hour of thought and reflection to reach it.'

The English Catholic writer and convert Christopher Hollis quotes in his autobiography a conversation which he had with the famous Hilaire Belloc. Belloc was a militant Catholic apologist if ever there was one. This is the faith, he would have said, take it or leave it. And yet, in a conversation with Hollis, he once said: 'The faith is never truly held unless it is held in challenge. The young man must get rid of what he has been merely taught and then rediscover it for himself. If he doesn't do that it isn't really his. It's not worth having.'

This was not an attitude which I found in plenty in Irish people talking about their faith in the 1970s. But things are improving.

🐵 🐵 🐵

There is one great peril to be met with in the life of the preacher, the teacher or the retreat director and that is the danger of becoming stale, flat, routine. Not only in one's heart and spirit but in the very way one says what one says and in the deadly certainty with which this is communicated to others. I began 'giving' or 'conducting' sisters' and priests' retreats while I was still in the Philippines. My first nuns' retreat was preached to Irish Mercy Sisters in Tacloban in the early 1960s. They had started their fine work there from St Marie's of the Isle, Cork. I have been part of more sisters' and priests' retreats since then than I care to remember. And there is no work in a retreat master's life which spoils him more: the audience is not only captive but sympathetic and friendly to a degree which one has to experience to really appreciate. But there is no obstacle to the onward creep of boredom and flatness. This is countered, often, in the lives of secular, educational people by research, field-work, experimentation. In the world of popular spirituality there is much less room for manoeuvre.

Then the Good Lord (I hope!) came to the rescue. My eye caught the review of a book (it was 1976) which struck me as just a little more than interesting. I bought it. The book was *Tensions: Necessary Conflicts in Life and Love* by H. A. Williams. No other book has helped me more than this nor lit more brightly my way forward; and very often my way of helping others as well. One thing it certainly did: it countered considerably, by the very nature of its message, the leaning or tendency to staleness or flatness both in myself or in those who had to listen to me.

* * *

Let me begin with the book's title – *Tensions*. Words are always a problem. They light up in our minds concepts and understandings which are commonly associated with the words but may not be the meaning which the speaker or writer has in mind, in fact, not the correct meaning of the word at all. 'Tension' is a good example. The popular meaning of tension would be trouble, unease, stress, unpleasant atmosphere, a by-product of unhappy personal relations.

Once, after speaking on this very subject, an elderly sister said to me in the sacristy: 'Thank God, Father, you said all that. There is fierce tension in this community.' Not exactly what I had in mind.

So, why use a word laden with associations? Because it is the best word to hand, it best conveys the idea in mind. That idea is the action-reaction, tug and counter-tug, the creative dynamism which is part of all life. I know nothing about science, chemistry or biology, but I do know that the smallest molecular particle gets its dynamic movement from the fact that it consists of a negative and positive charge, with tension, and therefore movement, between them.

You might use the word 'balance' but it carries too great a sense of repose. Or you might use the word 'conflict' but it carries overtones of victory or defeat. The word 'tautness' has its problems, too, as has the word 'pull'. Nothing conveys the idea of dynamism or aliveness as well as the word 'tension'.

Examples always help. There is an obvious tension or activity within all of us between the 'head' and the 'heart'. The head stands, figuratively, in popular acceptance, for being sensible, orderly, logical, knowing one's mind, putting one's foot down. The heart stands for sensitivity, feeling, forgiveness, making of allowances, 'having a little heart about us'. These are two very different ways of living but they are within each of us, they react one on the other, they are in tension. In order to to be fully human we have to relate one to the other, and the different ways in which we do this makes us, each person, different from the next person.

Or take the example of the feminine and the masculine *in each one of us*. We are masculine in the popular sense: active, dominant, logical, aggressive, protective. We are feminine in the sense of being gentle, accepting of love, able to give it, having a sense of the beauty and fragility of life, imaginative, perhaps a little illogical. These, again, are two very different ways of living but they are within us, they are in tension. We have to give them play – that is, if we want each person to be fully human. A third example might not be adverted to as easily as the others: the tension or pull between the imagination and the intellect or thinking, reasoning power. The intellect is cold, realistic, without much warmth, striving after logic and sense; the imagination is colourful, creative, builds castles in the air, produces a great deal of nonsense, but without it life would be very dull. Again, two different approaches to life. They have to be related, helped to strike one off the other. They are in tension and it has to be given healthy play.

All this becomes very clear when we see what happens (in any of these examples) if we 'collapse' this healthy tension and inter-play. In the heart-head tension one could give way completely to the 'head'. Then you have a certain kind of person: logical, efficient, unfeeling, sometimes ruthless, self-righteous, impossible to live with. Or one can become all heart: unreal, over-sensitive, foolish, letting others and events run away with one. Again, a pretty pathetic person.

In the male-female tension a person could become all male: rough, uncouth, insensitive, the plain blunt man. C. S. Lewis wrote in one of his letters: 'There ought to be a man in every woman and a woman in every man. And how horrid the ones are who have not got it. I can't bear a man's man or a woman's woman.' Many an Irish marriage has gone to pieces because people have not understood this.

In the imagination-intellect tension we can have collapse too. Then you end up with people who are all imagination: living in another world, no idea of what's happening on the ground, full of fancy and daydreams, in cloud-cuckoo land. Or one can be so caught up in the facts, the literal letter of the law, the 'right thing' to do, but having lost all sense of intuition or concession or balance. Another sick person.

I was not remotely interested in this line of thought because of any attraction of popular versions of psychology or psychiatry or psychoanalysis. They don't, in fact, attract me. While I believe that they have been of great help to some people they have done harm in certain ways. (I offer apologies, of course, to the professionals in that field for using very crude and, I'm sure, inexact terms.) But I did see, as I began to understand this book, *Tensions*, how its approach could make people marvellously alert, thoughtful, prayerful, creative and could, as H. A. Williams demonstrated, have profound effects on the spiritual life (its understanding and practice) in whole areas like prayer, chastity, obedience, poverty, penance, tradition – the difficult areas in fact.

* * *

A very healthy tension in spirituality (in the broad sense) is found in the interplay between the past and the present or future. Or to put it more formally, between traditional values and the prophetic vision. This is a vital tension to hold and we pay a heavy price when it has collapsed. H. A. Williams wrote (in one of his very few angry judgments): 'Those who are *exclusively* concerned to defend traditional values and those who are *exclusively* concerned with throwing them to the winds in the name of prophetic insight, have at least this in common: the moral indignation with which they receive criticism is matched only by the moral recklessness with which they inflict it' (p. 53).

As Pope John Paul wrote 'Prophecy comes out of memory'. Our roots are sustained by the past, we need its wisdom. Jesus said: 'I have not come to destroy the law but to fulfil it.' If we dump the past with all it has to tell us, we can very soon become lost. When Peter Hebblethwaite wrote his insightful book, *The Runaway Church*, he gave a good picture of what actually began to happen after Vatican II; it continues apace. We must recover the past and hold it in balance against the future or we are lost. Unomuno wrote: 'We live in memory and by memory and our spiritual life is at bottom the effort of our memory to persist, to transform itself into hope, the effort of our past to transform itself into our future.'

* * *

One tension today which we are particularly unwilling to hold is that between questioning and certainty. In the world of spiritual things, we don't actually have much certainty about anything, but we do have enough to go on. This tension, at its most profound and healthy level, is the tension between doubt and faith. Not that faith means certainty. St Paul tells us we walk by faith and not by sight – which would solve all our problems: we would then see. But let us take this tension in its simplest form, that between questioning and the reasonable amount of certainty which we have. It is good to ask questions, to have an open mind, 'to interiorise', to challenge. The scientific approach to education today makes questioning very natural. But it can become a kind of way of life, it can become the action of the swimmer treading water. Unfortunately one remains in the same place if one does nothing else and eventually one sinks. In the world of faith, of the religious life, this can happen. Cardinal Hume wrote in *Searching For God*: 'We live in an age of protest, an age of questioning. Now much of this is good but if it is to be an integral part of monastic life then I, for one, think that this life has no future.'

It is indeed quite clear that the collapse of this tension is very serious for anyone interested in the future. Questions and doubts are healthy but they must be offset by the light and the hope and the courage which are also our possession:

Lead kindly light, amid the encircling gloom
Lead thou me on...
Keep thou my feet; I do not ask to see
The distant scene; one step enough for me.

On the other hand we must not seek or demand too much certainty. So-called 'conservatives' tend to do this. They boast of their certainty, they claim to be above doubt, never, it seems, having reflected on or adverted to a warning such as that in the line of George MacDonald: 'The man that feareth, Lord, to doubt, in that fear doubted thee.'

But it is above all in moral matters, in questions to do with right and wrong, that the collapse of this tension is most far-reaching. People want certainty in moral matters, they demand black and white answers. 'Be honest, Father, which is it, yes or no?' We heard that question before somewhere: 'Master, you are an honest man; you teach in all honesty the way of life that God requires. Give us your ruling on this; are we or are we not permitted to pay taxes to the Roman Emperor?' (Mt 22). They got their answer. That answer contained enough tension between questioning and certainty to keep us going for two thousand years. But the collapse of this tension still goes on and we have to be repeatedly alerted to it. The leading American theologian C. S. Curran has rightly said that the demand for certainty by some people, especially in moral matters, is an albatross around the neck of the teaching Church.

* * *

There are two occasions when the secular media push the Church and its affairs on to the front pages or the front pictures. Some would say these are the only two times. One of them is any involvement of the Church in the world of sex, either in statement, practice or protest. The other occasion is any clash or argument between the Magisterium of the Church and the theologians. And here we have full play given to the media's love of labels: 'conservative', 'reactionary', 'liberal'. As if the Church then were in trouble – which is nonsense. One of the most healthy signs in the life of the Church is the enduring tension, well held, between the teaching Church and its thinkers, between the Pastoral Office and the Theological Office. This relationship has always been marked by 'collisions and contrasts'.

In a moving letter to the London *Times*, now over twelve years ago, Cardinal Hume wrote: 'How do we reconcile the right and duty of the theologian to pursue his researches in academic freedom with… the limitations of the human mind to discover truths about God which always lie beyond its compliance? The responsibility of the teaching authority within the Church to safeguard the authentic teaching of the Christian Gospel has to be maintained and, at the same time, the duty of the theologian to speculate has to be asserted. From time to time the two will clash; better this than indifference and apathy.'

This was a favourite line of thought with John Henry Newman. He would even have the tension held in play from three directions. The titles of prophet, priest and king which tradition ascribes primarily to Christ and, by extension, to the Church, form three functions in a delicate balance. In our post-Vatican II world we might put it this way: in the community of worship or the People of God you have the priestly function; in the doctrinal positions worked out or proposed by the theologians you have the prophetic role; in the government or administration of the Church, you have the kingly role. Simply, worship, theology and government are all essential to Catholicism. These three 'interests' (as Newman called them) must be held in creative tension. All of which can be seen a little better if we collapse this tension, let any one of these 'interests' fall down. Unhelped, unwatched prayer and devotion can become pure superstition. Unchecked, free-wheeling theology can lead to rationalism or worse. If there are no 'curbs' or 'stays' on government the danger could be tyranny. As a matter of fact, Newman had no doubt that the greatest danger in his time was ecclesiastical tyranny. We have to be thoughtful in our time.

A little understanding of all of this (by all of us) would be a great help. We would make more sense in thinking and talking about what is happening to us today, to our Church and to ourselves.

* * *

In giving this thought to the subject of healthy tensions I am not just presenting a book by H. A. Williams. Most of what I have said is not in the book at all. It is, in fact, a very short publication of less than 120 pages. But it was the direction in which it led that was most helpful. As a beginner, speaking to or talking with religious, one tended just to state the case. Their life, for example, rests on the three vows: poverty, chastity and obedience. You say what is permitted and what is not. You put exhortation, encouragement and inspiration as attractively as you can. But you cannot go much further.

What of the individuals themselves? What of their God-given gifts of initiative, of loving, of appreciation, of creativity? Do they mean nothing? Is it all about suppression or the forbidden? Or is it about a fullness of life? Take the vow of chastity or celibacy. Unless one brings into it something like the idea of a healthy tension one is very soon at a dead end. There is a tension there but sexuality is so sensitive an area in our living that the tension is swiftly 'collapsed'. We have all heard the phrase 'loveless chastity' – and met it. Or cynical remarks like 'the vow of chastity begins with loving God and ends with loving nobody'. But we are about love. As human beings we need to love and be loved, to know friends and friendship. The life of a saint like Teresa of Avila or John of the Cross would teach us this. On the one hand there is the God to whom we have dedicated our lives in love and 'a jealous God' but, on the other hand, to be true to what is best in us and most alive as human beings, we need human love. There are not many good works of fiction which deal with this but there is one: *In This House of Brede* by Rumer Godden. In the novel there is a marvellous scene where the dedicated sister stumbles on this truth: she needed human love. It was going to clash with her love of God but it was not going to destroy it. It was going to give that extraordinary dedication to God (the religious life) a new life, a spirit, a thoughtfulness, a prayerfulness and an agony. But it was going to save her. Of all the tensions in the life of the religious this one is the best.

Then you have the vow of poverty and, very often today, the idealising of it, the romanticising of it. There is nothing good whatever about poverty, hunger or want in themselves. They are a denial of the fatherhood of God. We all need food, clothes, comfort, security. On the other hand, there is the call of greed, gluttony, hedonism and selfishness. There is, in other words, a tension. It is only in holding that tension – between a decent frugality and materialism – that we make our practice of poverty real and responsible. If we don't place this idea of religious poverty in some such setting as that of tension it can very soon degenerate into the unreal and the phoney; as can be seen in some approaches to, or expressions of, the concept of identification with the poor.

In the whole world of obedience and authority, religious men and women have made great strides since Vatican II. They are far ahead, incidentally, of their brothers in the diocesan clergy. We have been exercising, in obedience, this process of healthy tension. On the one hand, superiors have to plan, give directions, dispose, appoint, decide. On the other hand the Spirit speaks in each of us, the spirit of freedom. That Spirit has to be listened to, appreciated, heard. There is a fruitful tension here between 'superior' and 'subject', between law and freedom. It is happily being worked out in religious orders and congregations none too badly. If one of the roles of the religious is to be a witness let us hope and pray that that witness is seen and read by others who need to see and heed.

* * *

I am not sure in talking about this very energising process of the healthy tension, that we might always realise how hard, difficult it is. We can never use the word 'easy' in its regard. As H. A. Williams said, in concluding his book: 'Our theme has been the Way of the Cross, that losing of our life to find it which takes the form of those necessary and health-giving conflicts which are the price we have to pay for becoming more fully ourselves.'

We do, indeed, in agonising over many a tension, have to slog along on foot, as it were. Often the most harrowing thing is not that the road is either rough or steep but that, as Jesus said, it is so narrow. Which might best be put in the words of the American writer Thornton Wilder: 'All the worthwhile things in life have to be fought for on a razor's edge and fought for everyday.'

Is there any resolving of our tensions this side of the grave? There is not. Perhaps the supreme help offered us, either by nature or grace, is a sense of humour. To be able, in our predicaments, to laugh at ourselves (as well as at others) goes a long way. The truest of all stock phrases, it has been said, is 'saved by a sense of humour'.

Maybe the poets and the mystics have come nearest to the truth. Their feeling is that only in heaven do we have the resolving of our tensions. In John Donne's beautiful prayer, he says that only there (in heaven) do we find reconciliation: between silence and noise, between music and discord, between the end and the beginning.

In his excellent book *Introducing the Christian Faith* the saintly Michael Ramsey wrote: 'In heaven the antitheses which so often disturb us will be resolved. Worship and service will be one. Activity and rest will find harmony. The triumph of achievement and the fascination of new discovery will be blended.'

🐜 🐜 🐜

One of the early points of growth in the life of a priest or preacher, of anyone indeed, comes when it is realised that one's enthusiasm (for anything) does not always find a response in others. When I began speaking to priests and religious I used to give a separate and what I considered an important lecture on reading. Any reading to begin with, but spiritual reading in the main. This was accompanied by a list of books which I had either read myself or knew enough about. I would not now be caught dead doing any such thing. There are easier ways of doing good or harm!

First of all, any choice or recommendation in reading is arbitrary. It is very personal. Some of the greatest books in the world do not appeal to everyone. I have never been able to relate to one of the most famous of them: *The Imitation of Christ.* I made at least two attempts to read *The Story of a Soul* by Thérèse of Lisieux. I simply could not take it. Which is not to say that it is not a great book. I am glad to make amends by adding that Thérèse's letters, translated by Frank Sheed, were and remain for me a great spiritual help.

An individual recommendation, of course, is always welcome and we should do more of it. Not so long ago I was looking along the shelves in a bookshop in Dublin. I moved on a little further to find myself beside a priest who had a book in his hand. He was leafing through it thoughtfully. I said to myself: That man is going to spend £15 on that book, and it is not worth 15 pence. I had read it. I took the chance (as courteously as I could) to get talking with him and told him what I thought. He shot the book back on the shelf. 'Thanks be to God', he said and added, laughing, 'You find robbery in every shape and form these times.' We had a cup of coffee together.

Why do people read so little today? It is an interesting question against the background of growing lists of new titles every year, to say nothing of growing numbers of good book shops. This does not, as one might imagine, signify growing numbers of new readers. In the UK 85 per cent of all books sold are bought by only 15 per cent of the population. However, coming in at a narrow point in a complex question, it has to be agreed that the culture of our time does not encourage the reading habit. We are very much immediate people. We want things presented now, canned, ready-made, in tabloid form, the brief image, the sound-bite, the slogan, banner theology. This is our day; the long, often tedious reading time, the concentration, the imagination, even the patience of sympathy are seldom there. And the counter-attractions are the radio, the TV, the video, a world of image and colour; and the reflection of all this is the very professional presentation of the mass media papers.

Still I believe that wide, general reading, sacred or secular, is of very great importance, certainly for the priest or preacher. The fruits of broad reading can add a great deal to the presentation of the Good News. It can give width, depth, illustration, colour to what one is saying. It can do a lot to link the spiritual message to our humanity, to our time and place. All of which can be seen or rather heard in the speaking and preaching of the good general reader: illustration, humour, perspective, comparison. Historians point out that even the ancient Fathers of the Church owe their theological excellence in no small measure to their pagan education. Their minds were not corrupted in their schools but rather broadened.

The opposite is also sadly true and it has to be said. Quite a large number of younger preachers today present the message in rather bald forms. Their sole method of emphasis is very often sheer repetition. Their store of illustration or example or comparison is small. If they did not have, for background, the perennial concept of boy-girl love or if they did not have to hand the plight of the poor and marginalised, one wonders how they would say what they want to say or what they would say at all: the direct result of being badly or poorly read.

There is one point at which general reading plays a vital role, especially today. We are living in a world of movements: the great prayer movement, feminism, the charismatic renewal, fundamentalism. These movements can take people over completely. Balance and emphasis are lost – some of these movements are in essence an imbalance! No call or movement, for example, was more needed than feminism. No group was more unacceptably treated than women in State and Church and, yet, we have signs around that the movement is being undertorn, even wrecked, on its own wilder shores. Balance is being lost. A little reading would have prevented this.

The great prayer movement has made a successful and wide appeal to the modern heart and mind. But the deadly concentration on just some aspects of prayer, the hijacking of other areas of it by popular psychology or pseudo-mysticism, the adulation of well-advertised proponents of one prayer-form or another – all this has done great harm to and even shrunk that most fascinating and varied of all our forms of relating to the mystery of God: prayer. Again, good general reading on the subject would have saved the day.

The most serious of all the imbalances in the world of movements, however, is found in the charismatic renewal. And the problem, again, lies in the lack of good literature and reading on the Holy Spirit. Any attempt to confine our devotion to the Pentecost, to singing and celebrating and alleluias is a profound mistake. There are no short-cuts to God. No one can avoid the searching or the tears or the cross or our death. We are Paschal Mystery people as well as Pentecostal people. As Von Hugel said: 'It is folly to attempt the finding of a shorter way to God than the closest contact with his own coming down.' Because of a failure in general reading, you have these attempts to understand Christian spirituality as an experience apart from the historical events of our redemption. We must never forget the central challenge: 'It is a costly thing to invoke the Spirit, for the glory of Calvary was the cost of the Spirit's mission and is the cost of the Spirit's renewal. It is in the shadow of the cross that in any age in history Christians pray: Come thou holy Paraclete.'

* * *

Books don't appeal to everyone, certainly not the same books. Standards of judgement and criticism vary. We are living now in a world of 'best-sellers', of prize-winners, of million dollar sales. Between the two world wars, before the best-seller lists arrived, the world of books (certainly in English) was headed by a few names. For almost twenty years (in the 1920s and 1930s) the top three were well and truly tried: the Bible, *The*

Imitation of Christ and *The Story of San Michele* by Axel Munthe. Standards have tumbled since then. Perhaps Marilyn Monroe's comment on Hollywood applies all round: 'They give you $50,000 for a kiss and 50 cents for your soul.'

How do we judge a book? There is certainly wisdom and help for countless readers in the answer given by Samuel Johnson. He claimed that the worth of a work of literature can be assessed in only one way: 'No other test can be applied', he said, 'than the esteem, its length and continuance, which has surrounded the book.'

When I became a major seminarian in 1945 novels, as already mentioned, were forbidden, except during holidays. An air of disapproval, almost disrepute, surrounded them. Even though fiction, together with poetry, has always been the high moment and glory of the great literatures of the world. In the closed existence of religious in the 1940s novels were a danger, a temptation, a call to worldliness and frivolity. Fiction was certainly not seen as an opening up, as a view or a vision of the human heart with all its problems, Few then would have understood the advice of Robin Lloyd Jones, 'If you want to know what poverty and injustice are really like only fiction can give you the truth.'

I once asked a priest who lived in South Africa what was worthwhile reading on the tortured story of apartheid. He said, 'Read the novels of Alan Paton, *Too late the Phalarope* and especially his truly wonderful book *Cry the Beloved Country*.' I did and am gratefully in his debt.

We sometimes indulge in the Desert Island game. What books would you take with you if you were to be stranded and have nothing else to read for the rest of your life? (Generations are coming 'on stream' now who would bring none, of course, but I am indulging myself!) I am sure that the books which helped one most – spiritually or psychologically – would be high on the list. But could you continue to read them? Very unlikely. The real test is the re-read: the book you can live with, the book which presents a world, as nature does, in which you can take a walk now and then, see different things, feel differently, have space, be strangely at home. There are not many of these on the list of the ordinary, general reader, but let's hope there are some. For myself, apart from the Bible which has its own unique place, I should select: *The Confessions of Augustine, The Canterbury Tales*, Shakespeare, Newman's *Apologia Pro Vita Sua, The Path to Rome* by Hilaire Belloc and Robin Flower's translation of *The Islandman* by Tomás Ó Cróhan. I cannot be specific in my reasons for this choice but those reasons go back in the end, I'm sure, to what literature is about: partly nostalgia, partly atmosphere, partly that evening light which falls across the pages of the classics, partly love, partly one's youth and partly a feeling of failure in the sense in which J. M. Barrie used the word when he said, 'We are all failures, especially the best of us.'

& & &

In his excellent but controversial biography of St Thomas More, Richard Marius writes: 'For all their zeal and virtue the Utopians possessed a Christian sense of limitation. It was More's sense. He had a strong apocalyptic view, perfection for the world would come only when Christ came again. In the meantime we must take what goodness we can find, without straining for the impossible. Every monk stood in a corrupt world which imposed boundaries even on what virtuous men and women could do; so did every Utopian.'

As I tried over the years to help others and myself, through preaching or writing or trying to pray, I came slowly, sadly to realise the central importance of what Thomas More was saying in his famous book *Utopia*. It is very necessary for people to have right attitudes in order to learn to grow as children of God; it is very important that the spiritual life be lifted, even kept alive, prayerful and alert with some such idea as that of healthy tensions; it is very basic that people read and keep their minds balanced and refreshed, but over all, or rather under all, runs the fault-line: limitations. We are a broken world. Lurking around always are the traps, the limitations: evil, selfishness, sin. There, as Thomas Hardy pointed out, is the duty of the poet and the novelist: to show the grandeur underneath the sorriest of things and the sorriest of things beneath the grandeur. It is also the duty of the preacher and the priest.

* * *

We are limited in all we can do by our sinfulness. We have had, it is true, as Catholics, too great an emphasis on sin. A great deal of our preaching in the past was moralistic and preachers today have genuinely tried to get away from too legalistic and minimalist approaches to living the Christian life. But the sinfulness remains, which we must not forget. Forms of Revelation express themselves in apocalyptic terms – beating swords into ploughshares, reaching for the new heaven and the new earth – which can tempt us to forget that, like the poor, sin will always be with us, with each one.

Some of the theologies which have taken hold of the modern Church needed to be warned about. The very attractive 'theology of the secular city' is a good example. It played an important role in helping to break down the barriers between the secular and the sacred but it has been described recently, and rightly, as 'an horrendously narrow vision'. The 'secular city' was sinful and imprisoned two-thirds of the earth in hunger, misery and want. Our friend

Liberation Theology stands in judgment: side by side with the desire and hope of harmony, justice and liberation lurk selfishness, jealousy and pride.

Not so long ago, in a report from the Philippines, the New People's Army was welcomed in the *barrios* (poor communities). It set out to remove the glaring abuses of the thieves, the Government soldiers. But then, in its turn, the NPA became demanding and arrogant, shooting people without trial. 'The evils of our proud and angry dust are from eternity and shall not fail.'

In the quiet of the confessional, in the gentle atmosphere of the spiritual director's room, one has so often to place a hand on the shoulder of another and say: 'Be patient, leave it in God's hands, we labour and are burdened.' It is only in a true feel for our own sinfulness that we can hope to grow to goodness. I only wish I learned this sooner.

* * *

We are limited, bound by time, though we always try to beat it. We seem unable to absorb the wisdom of the Russian proverb: 'Do not rush things, let them be born.' We accuse the pre-Vatican II Church of being triumphalist and fall into a triumphalism of our own. We want things to happen quickly, we call for, expect a 'reception' of the teachings of the Council overnight, when in fact – at least according to Karl Rahner – it will take a hundred years. The Council of Trent took longer.

We try to persuade our listeners of the gospel message for today, forgetting that half of them are the men and women of yesterday. We try to tell the young how to live, how to be Christian now, forgetting that they are better prepared by their own time and better forewarned than we their elders are. We are of another time.

We think that there was and is only one time, our time. And so we have all the despondency and despair and fear in the face of change, novelty and loss when, of course, the Church has seen it all before, many times. I have just been reading of a twelfth century bishop and his cry: 'Why do so many novelties occur in the Church of God?'

There is no more favourite idea in discussion today than that of 'structures'. We want to get rid of bad ones, create new ones, forgetting that, of all the forms and helps in building human practice, the slowest to grow and be of use are structures. For to be of any help they must come out of how we see things, feel things, have loved things; and that takes a long, long time. I only wish, again, that I had learned all this much sooner.

* * *

We are hand-tied, limited by the complexity of things now. Looking back we are tempted to say that, in the past, life was simple, the options few, the decisions to be made and the advice to be offered more or less obvious. That is probably an illusion but there is no doubting it today: we are living in a puzzling world 'amid great multiplicity and complexity with myriad possibilities'. Modern science and expertise have opened up new vistas in physics, chemistry, biology, genetics. Choices are now placed before people against a background of experimentation in human fertility and embryonic research, choices which can only be described as daunting. They are certainly limiting.

There was a time when the Seventh Commandment – Thou Shalt Not Steal – was easily understood and preached. But we are now in a world of interlocking commerce with its forest of companies, subsidiaries, off-shore accounts, dense legal protection, and nowhere around any simple sign or proof that one man is stealing from another. What is the confessor to do? What is the Church to preach? Bernard Lonergan maintained that the primary crisis facing theology and the Christian life today is not a crisis of faith but a crisis of culture. There is a breakdown, he said, in the mediation of meaning. 'Judging and deciding are left to the individual and he finds his plight desperate. There is far too much to learn before he can begin to judge. Yet judge he must and decide he must if, he is to exist, if he is to be a man' (*Collected Papers*).

I have found all this very difficult, as every priest must. I have been very fortunate to live in Marianella community, a great number of whose members are teachers in the various disciplines, (scripture, moral theology, ecclesiology), lecturing in universities and major seminaries. One goes to them for help – having tried one's best to help oneself. Still we continue, often not to know what decisions to make or what advice to give. One finds comfort in the old story from Jesuit lore. The brilliant young priest was undergoing his final oral exam in Moral Theology. He knew everything, had all the answers. Finally, the old professor said, 'One more question, Father, what would you do if you did not know what to do?'

* * *

The English poet Laurie Lee wrote three books of autobiography, the first of which, *Cider with Rosie,* became very famous. In the third and most moving volume, *A Moment of War,* he tells of an incident in Spain. The book is about his experiences there during the terrible Civil War of the 1930s. Government soldiers – anti-Franco of course – would be billeted in the burned-out, devastated ruins of churches. But a powerful yet unwritten law held. Though a church was violated, mutilated, stripped, nobody went near the altar. For these hard-bitten men, a line was drawn surrounding the sacred stone. An angel seemed on guard: an invisibly marked area near which even the most ribald, profane and godless men did not go.

Laurie Lee takes up the story: 'As we stamped in from the slushy street, our clothes and ponchos soaking, each man bagged his personal patch of ground by throwing down his kit. The chapel filled rapidly, the territories staked out; but I hesitated as under a spell. The altar, beneath its tinted east window, was a stripped pedestal of stone and plaster, lightly washed in flaking blue paint. Quickly I went up to it, threw down my bags, stretched myself along it and lit a cigarette. With this gesture, this idiot impulse of brash bravado, I believe I stained the rest of my life.'

In this poignant and humble memory Laurie Lee puts his finger on the greatest of the limitations chaining us down – all of us: our past. We will not let it go. We allow the failures, the sins, supposedly forgiven, to continue to haunt us, shape us, stain our lives. After the healing words of the sacrament our sins are actually no more. But we do not believe it. An Irish Carmelite missionary home from Africa told me of his surprise hearing confessions there and the penitent saying 'I have no sins'. 'But you must have some sins. What about the past? Mention a sin of your past life.' But no, there were none. They had been forgiven, they were gone. No sins. That is what faith and hope are about. I certainly have not found that faith, certainly not that hope, in Israel!

🐜 🐜 🐜

No subject challenges the preacher like the subject of suffering. How on God's earth do you explain or defend or negotiate the terrible problem of pain? How do you reconcile a loving and compassionate God with a world of agony and woe? The simple answer is that you cannot do it. The question for the preacher is, does he believe that? Or can he make his hearers believe it?

What happens most times is this: the preacher starts (and sometimes goes on) with examples of suffering and tragedy – as if we needed examples. The words of the poet are deep in us: 'We were born in another's pain and shall perish in our own.' Examples and illustrations are, in an exact meaning of the words, a real waste of time: time which the preacher needs (in the usually short span at his disposal) to help himself and his listeners find some way, some approach, some stance by which suffering can have a meaning in the mysterious design which is the Christian life.

The very first thing we must do or say about suffering is to face it directly. There is nothing good about it, in spite of all the attempts around to romanticise it. Suffering is destructive and demeaning by its nature. If we let it, it will make us bitter, angry, vindictive and self-pitying. But we have been given, each one, a humanity and a dignity. In the face of pain we must keep faith with that dignity. As Dostoevsky prayed: 'There is only one thing I dread, not to be worthy of my sufferings.' With the natural virtues of acceptance, courage, patience and good humour we can walk with suffering and throw some light on God's presence there; for it was the Lord who gave us that humanity. It is the very first point at which our faith plays a part in the great mystery of pain.

And with that word 'mystery' we put our finger on the central fact about suffering: it is a mystery. No religion has an answer to pain. Not the Christian faith, nor any other. One of the great non-Christian religions has resorted, in part, to the famous and bizarre theory of the transmigration of souls. Suffering is punishment for, and cleansing from evil done in another existence. But even that theory fails to quiet human bewilderment in the face of pain. As Jesus died upon the cross, he cried out 'My God, my God, why have you forsaken me?' He did not get an answer. The great literary achievement of the Old Testament, the Book of Job, faced the problem and, as Chesterton commented, it found the answer to suffering: there is no answer. It remains a mystery.

So, has our faith nothing to say before suffering? It has. As the echoes of Jesus' cry 'My God, my God…' faded across the city he called out again, 'Into thy hands, O Lord, I commend my Spirit.' There is what our Faith has to say: in spite of everything, in spite of pain and fear, in spite of the destruction of wonderful people and things, there is a meaning to it all in God. We place the mystery in his hands. We trust our faith. In the end it is about hope. It was the answer Jesus gave to the question of pain; it was the answer he used himself. As Paul Claudel wrote: 'Jesus did not come to explain away suffering. He came to fill it with his presence.'

We can at a remove, be quite positive about suffering. It does, for example, help at times to remind ourselves that suffering (some of it at least) is the price we pay for free will: many a cross, many a pain, many a death is the result of you or me being free human beings – taking the wrong road and paying that price.

Then again pain can be a powerful teacher, a forming force in its own way for good. Cardinal Newman wrote: 'Nothing short of suffering can make us what we should be: gentle instead of harsh, meek instead of violent, conceding instead of arrogant, lowly instead of proud, pure-hearted instead of sensual, sensitive to sin instead of carnal.'

A final exercise, in the face of suffering, one that is imaginative and worthwhile, has helped some: reflection on what our world would be like if there were no suffering in it, no sorrows, no hardship, no cross, no agony, no risk. It would be an awful place for it would be a world without courage, without heroism, without leadership, without achievement or success, without greatness, without reward. In more senses than theological, there is a glory which surrounds the cross; we would all be the poorer without it.

A number of years ago I wrote (in *Reality* magazine) a short one-page reflection on the general idea of suffering. It was called 'The Cross of Christ'. I was merely making what I thought was an important distinction within the whole painful subject. For what it is worth, this is what I wrote:

One of the very best things we can do in life is to make clear distinctions. In fact countless miseries come about because of a lack of them, because of misunderstandings and confusion. Clear distinctions are as necessary and as powerful in the area of religion as anywhere else.

Take, for example, Easter, when we celebrate the Cross of Christ and his Resurrection. There is a distinction here which we might very profitably make. Indeed we may find, as a result, a challenge in that same Cross of Christ which we never found before.

And the distinction has to be made in using the very phrase: the Cross of Christ. We tend to use the words in a blanket sense. Everything we suffer or dislike we call a cross: ill health, failure, betrayal, redundancy, a difficult teenager. None of these are of course the Cross of Christ. They are nothing, be they great or small, nothing other than the ills to which all flesh is heir.

For the Cross of Christ, speaking in the strict and correct sense, is only that suffering or that burden or that sorrow faced by us because of our love of Christ and his message. When he bids us take up our cross and follow him he is not talking about the sorrows and sufferings which are part of all living. We have no choice but to carry them. Jesus is talking about the sufferings we might avoid if we were ready to forget him and take the easy way. When a doctor or a journalist loses promotion because he or she will not support abortion, when a girl loses her boyfriend because she will not commit fornication, when an official makes an enemy because he will not take a bribe – when all this and a lot more like it happens, then you see what is meant by the Cross of Christ. Then you see someone taking up that cross and following him.

And a very vital point: if we do not see and put into practice the distinction I am talking about we may go on carrying the ordinary (and often very heavy) burdens of life with a certain patience and acceptance and think thereby that we are being Christian, following in the footsteps of Christ. But his Cross demands much more. It demands things which would actually change you and me and our world. But we do not take up this Cross. That is why the mysterious dimension of failure and defeat which is part of the gloom of Good Friday still hangs around us; that is why the morning of His Resurrection still throws little of its light and glory into our heedless hearts.

The reaction I received to the above was instructive. One reader was very unhappy that I had made the distinction which I had made. It appears that I had upset her understanding of taking up the cross and following the Lord. She had come to terms with that call of the New Testament. She was bearing the burdens of life – that was what the Lord meant. But was it? For here we are at one of the centres of the mystery: we can never be content. Suffering keeps us on our toes, keeps us searching, keeps us 'alive', tells us that we have no hiding place. There is a beautiful set of Stations or Way of the Cross in Marianella chapel. Each picture of those stations is a different shape to remind us that the cross does not repeat itself. It is a new challenge each time, a new testing.

🐜 🐜 🐜

The French poet and mystic Charles Péguy puts these words in the mouth of God: 'I know man well… you can ask a lot of kindness of him, a lot of love, a lot of sacrifice. He has much faith and much charity. But what you cannot ask of him, by heavens, is just a little hope.'

I know, in my experience, of no words more true. I have never been scandalised by anything I ever encountered in the confessional or anywhere else. Indeed, my abiding overall impression, after many years, is of the essential goodness, even greatness of people. There is one exception: the absence of hope, of trust in God. Deep down in all of us, it seems, come hell or high water, is the belief, the determination, that we can make it on our own, that there is a way forward if we can only be helped to find it. To the advice – and so often the only advice possible – 'leave it with God', 'trust God', you get that glazed look which tells you you are wasting your time. Oscar Wilde was speaking for all of us, from Reading Gaol:

> *We did not dare to breathe a prayer*
> *Or give our anguish scope;*
> *Something was dead in all of us,*
> *And what was dead was hope.*

Most priests, at one time or another, must have asked themselves why there was this lack of hope, of trust in God. I did. Why has one of the central messages of the New Testament so failed to be part of Christian hearts and minds? Nobody can read, surely, or pray over, the Letters of Peter and Paul and not be touched by hope. Over the years I have learned by heart a whole series of texts from Romans, Colossians, Peter and Ephesians that I might have them to hand in helping others; I doubt if I did.

'The hope that awaits you in heaven was *the lesson* which you learned from the truth-giving message of the Gospel which has reached you' (Col 1:5).

'Blessed be God, the Father of Our Lord Jesus Christ, who in his great mercy has begotten us anew, making hope live in us, through the Resurrection of Jesus Christ from the dead' (1P 1:3).

'We are reconciled to God through his Son's death and, so reconciled are surer than ever of finding salvation' (Rm 5:10).

'It is God's grace that has saved you; raised us up too, enthroned us too above the heavens in Christ Jesus' (Ep 2:6).

An atheist like Lenin could say that the New Testament was the most dangerous book on earth because it was a book of hope; yet we cannot see it. Why?

It all goes back, I think, to one or more of the heresies which we might have thought long dead. Chesterton was right when he said that a heresy never dies. It only goes away and awaits its chance again, watching from its lair in hell.

Take the Pelagian heresy: it had its origins in a monk who lived 1,500 years ago, Pelagius. He taught that Original Sin, that basic flaw in men and women, does not exist, that God's help is not necessary, that we can earn heaven all by ourselves. St Augustine thought that he had destroyed this heresy. The Church, in the person of Pope Boniface II, decisively condemned it. But it lives on. Under the guise of a one-sided insistence on the necessity of personal 'good works' it was at least partially responsible for starting the Protestant Reformation. Listen to our sermons, our preoccupation with what we should do to merit this or merit that. Just listen to people. Pelagius is alive and well. The words of St John are forgotten: 'Nobody can come to me unless the Father who sent me draw him.' It is a very short step from depending totally on ourselves to losing hope in God; and that is how we have lost it.

But Pelagius is not the only gentleman from the past alive and well. The Pharisee still lives on. The Pharisees were good, even great people in the history of Israel. St Paul was a Pharisee and proud of it. But they were guilty of one central error. The Pharisee believed he was the architect, the builder, of his own salvation. He speaks of his justice, he never transgresses God's law, he plays his part. But God never finds in him the surrender, the opening, the need through which the Lord can enter and save. In the famous parable Jesus contrasts him with the publican who was humble, in need, who cried out and was answered. The publican trusted God, the Pharisee really only trusted in himself. We have met such everywhere.

It is interesting that St Thérèse of Lisieux came to her famous Way of Spiritual Childhood (that total trust of a child) through meditating on St Paul's criticism of the Pharisees. The mystics, of course, with their extraordinary intimacy with God, knew it all along. St Paul tells us that all things work together into good; Julian of Norwich said that all manner of things will be well, and Charles de Foucauld, writing from his desert hut, told his niece: 'The one thing we owe to Jesus is not to be afraid.'

Early on, hearing confessions, I got very good advice from a very good confessor. He said: 'Don't give too much advice to people in the confessional. Don't try to right too many wrongs. Just take one problem. Help the penitent in one area if you can. What you say may be remembered; if you throw the whole catechism at a man he will remember nothing!' For many years I have confined myself (with exceptions) just to helping people to renew or find a trust in God, to finding a little hope; it is, in the end, the healing of all our hurts.

For myself, I have made my own the prayer of Thomas Merton:

> *My Lord God: I have no idea where I am going. I do not see the road ahead of me. I cannot know for certain where it will end. Nor do I know myself: the fact that I think I am following your will does not mean that I am actually doing so. But, I believe that the desire to please you does in fact please you. And I hope I have that desire in all that I am doing. I hope I will never do anything apart from that desire. And I know that if I do this you will lead me by the right road though I may know nothing about it. Therefore, will I trust you always though I may seem to be lost and in the shadow of death. I will not fear, for you are with me; and you will never leave me to face my perils alone.'*

* * *

On the evening of 30 September 1975 I got a message from the provincial superior. He wanted to see me after supper for a moment. True to form, Fr Jim McGrath gave me an expansive welcome. The office was full of smiles. He had good news – he didn't say for whom – and I waited. 'We have decided', he went on (nobody could use the royal 'we' so well) ,'to appoint you editor of *Reality*, in charge of Redemptorist Publications.' I don't know what expression I registered but it did not deter Fr Jim. 'As we see it', he continued, 'you will do a very good job.' Finding my voice, I said, 'Fr Jim, could I think about it for a bit?' 'Oh no', he said, with disarming friendliness, 'we have sent your name out in the post this evening. Could you begin in the morning?' I began in the morning.

The *Redemptorist Record* was started in November 1936. The magazine's first editor, Fr Tom Murphy, was a Kerryman, born in Brosna in 1878. Fr Tom was not only a gifted writer but a fanatic in his belief in the power of the written word. He never stopped writing. The account of his life, provided by tradition for the Redemptorist archives, says that in old age the pen literally fell from his hand.

The *Record* began publication in Belfast with a modest print-run of 8,000. Its offices remained in the North till 1962, when they came south to Dublin. In the beginning the magazine was bi-monthly, only coming out every month from 1964. The years of the Second World War were very difficult for all non-essential publications, as paper was so scarce, but the *Redemptorist Record* survived throughout.

The original aims of the magazine were put very clearly in the first editorial. They are not only of historical interest, but have continued to bear influence right up to the present – not always to the advantage of those who later came to carry on Fr Tom's work.

The aims were: firstly, the defence 'by every means in our power', of the teaching of the Church in a world where there was such 'a violent, widespread and ill-informed attack on the sacred teaching of our Saviour'. The second aim was to uphold and continue the legacy of St Alphonsus whose pen was ever busy and whose books and booklets issued from the press in a never-ending stream. Thirdly, the magazine was to present and support the Redemptorist Foreign Mission in the Philippines. 'Many people,' wrote the Editor, 'would help this foreign missionary work if they knew of its existence and the conditions of it. But they do not.' Fr Tom himself had spent eleven years in the Far East.

In October 1965 the name *Redemptorist Record* was changed. The magazine became *Reality*. Behind the change of name and, with it, change of direction, was another Kerryman, Fr Michael O'Connor. It is interesting to note in passing that names don't die too easily. Thirty years after the change of the title, older subscribers, even confrères, continue to refer to *The Record*.

It was 1965. Vatican II had done its paperwork. It was now to be implemented. What Fr O'Connor actually did was to 'go national'. Up to that time the *Record* was really The *Redemptorist* Record. The achievements, the hopes, the needs of the Congregation were foremost: and foremost, especially the reporting on the foreign missions – never, by the way, presented in a trivial, over-romantic or 'black baby' manner. Indeed the *Redemptorist Record*, especially in the ten years under Fr Tom Murphy, had not only a very high content quality but a very high literary standard as well. Fr Tom got some of the best people around in history, journalism and fiction to write for him, like Dr Helena Concannon, Alice Curtayne, Dr Eoin MacNeill, Annie M. P. Smithson.

But the Church and the world were changing. New ideas, new directions, new challenges were upon us. People needed to be helped, encouraged, re-educated. It was a Church in renewal. No publication, around that time, could remain faithful to its best self if it did not change, if it did not face the questions being asked, if it did not go where the need was greatest. Fr Michael O'Connor did just that.

How successful was the early *Reality*? Reading over the letters in file in the ten years up to 1975, it is clear that *Reality* did a good job. It was recognised as 'serious', 'relevant', 'readable', 'up-to-date', 'badly needed'. It was mentioned in Dáil debates and (a sure sign of hitting targets) it was involved in controversy – with both Church and State.

Looking back over the years from 1936 to 1975 the

magazine of the Redemptorists (whatever its name) was faithful to its mission, as it saw it at the time. With the exception of a number of years in the 1950s, when there was an over-concentration on sex and sexual morality (at its worst) the magazine kept a high standard, it served the Church well, it met real needs, it was not afraid of problems. It was, in fact, true to the mission of that wonderfully gifted man, its first editor. And he would have nodded in eager agreement with the words of the modern prophet Solzhenitsyn: 'It is infinitely difficult to begin where mere words must move a great block of inert matter. But there is no other way, if none of the material strength is on your side. And a shout in the mountains has been known to start an avalanche.'

🐜 🐜 🐜

I came to the Editor's Office on 1 October, 1975. I shall always remember my first phone call. It was from our printers in Drogheda, in the person of a Mr Enda Hughes. We were to come to know each other very well. Enda was an excellent man at his job but he had not yet met anyone in publishing quite as raw as myself. After welcoming me to *Reality* he said, 'Father, we are about to print. (It was the November issue.) I am puzzled about the op-ed. The instructions on it read: Range left, dropped capitals. It looks funny to me. There doesn't seem to be a lower case anywhere…'. 'Listen, Enda,' I said, 'Wait a minute. I don't know what an op-ed is. I don't know what a range is – right or left! I never heard of dropped capitals and I have no idea what a lower case might be… .' I was interrupted by Enda's hearty laugh. 'Don't worry, Father, we'll fix things. We'll do it together.' We did. But it was from that far back I had to start.

Starting for most people, including myself, would normally mean doing some thinking on what one was about to embark on, in this case, considering what the magazine was for or should be for. Almost immediately I was down to something much more concrete and tangible: money. It was a question of survival. *Reality* was being heavily subsidised. It was not remotely paying its way. Its circulation figures were quite unreal. An unsettling phrase like 'paid sales' was hardly ever heard. Apart from a very efficient manager, nobody gave a thought to costs: paper, wages, printing, design, illustration, bad debts: free copies all round. When we got too far into the red for comfort the provincial bursar came to the rescue. It was to take a long time to solve, at least partially, the money crisis and that thanks to the help and advice of a friend, a professional finance man. Then there was circulation; it was, and remains, a crucial problem.

* * *

When one talks about the circulation of a magazine one usually begins with figures. As I am unable to absorb more than a few of them I will not impose them on anyone else. The general picture is that circulation figures of religious papers and magazines are falling everywhere. According to the latest statement in the Irish Marketing Surveys Report, 50 per cent of the population of Ireland at the moment read no religious or Church literature of any kind. The reason given by 50 per cent of them is that they are just not interested or find them boring. Incidentally, a more disconcerting fact (from the same report) is that the typical reader of *Reality* magazine would be: female, married, between fifty and sixty-four years of age, whose husband is from the middle/lower class. This fact is disconcerting for a very simple reason. *Reality* has made a special effort over the years to deal with the problems and questions concerning youth, education, preparation for marriage, drugs, the rearing of children, the finding of a vocation in life, suicide, crime and so on – but all to little avail, it appears, if the people to whom the publication is speaking are nowhere around. There are limitations, obviously, to the claim that if, in your magazine, you meet the needs of people, respond to the questions they are asking, you will have the readers. One wonders.

Why are circulation figures falling? Reading in general is falling. We have not even begun to absorb the impact of an audio, audio-visual world. It will take some time to discover to what extent the written word survives, though survive one hopes it will.

In the case of *Reality* you had the change of name and nature which, even up to now, has not commended itself *fully* to Redemptorists. People have often said to me: you have a marvellous selling instrument in all the Redemptorist missions, retreats, novenas and churches around the country. Let me say just this: whatever grace-filled gifts the good Lord gave the Redemptorists, and he gave them many and I am proud to be part of them, the same Lord did not give many of them a publisher's heart or a printer's soul. They are not great sellers. For one thing, the thought of promoting or selling 'our own magazine' is off-putting for many of them. Looking at just one figure: in the year 1983, with a circulation in one month of 27,000 copies, only 1,120 were sold in our churches and retreat centres. I think ruefully of another great body of men working in the Irish Church. The members of that Society jump into the market place to sell their own wares: books, magazines, periodicals, pamphlets. And the result: they have been in the forefront of Church publications in Ireland for 150 years.

There are further reasons for the fall in circulation. The lessening of the foreign missionary content did not help

Reality. The traditional outlets and means of selling are disappearing: the churches are closed for a great deal of the day. Religious, especially sisters, are fewer, religiously committed teachers are not as many as they were. Our promoters – that marvellous body of people – are getting fewer. These had all been great helpers. We have often heard the phrase 'the accepted wisdom'. Sometimes it is wisdom. But you have also 'the accepted nonsense' and it is nearly always nonsense. You hear, for example, comments (very often from priests) which state: 'Ah sure, nobody would read much in this parish.' Or 'Ah, *Reality* is a bit too difficult for the ordinary person'. Once in a fit of desperation I carried out a rough-and-ready survey of a hundred scattered readers. Not one of them (they were asked specifically) said that it was too difficult. We put our finger here on a very tender spot in the world of communicating the Good News of God. We don't just underestimate people in their ability to understand and make ideas their own; we lack real respect for them. As a thoughtful politician like Adlai Stevenson could say: 'The average man [and woman] is a good deal better than the average. They should be treated more often with intellectual respect.'

🐾 🐾 🐾

Most magazines and Church papers in Ireland are members of the Religious Press Association, founded in Dublin in the mid-1960s. With a small executive committee it has been of considerable service to everyone involved in the field. At the moment it has a membership of thirty-four publications, although there are more titles than that in the country. Indeed one of the problems is just here: we have too many religious magazines in Ireland. And to add to the overcrowding, since

Ireland is an English-speaking country religious literature pours in from abroad: Britain, the US, Canada, Australia. With the strange (even weird) belief that as Ireland is mainly Catholic it is therefore a reading population (!) one or two of the huge-circulation, continental magazines (like *Familia Cristiana* in Italy) have given consideration to English language editions – to add to our woes!

The difficulties in rationalising the Church magazine scene here are considerable. For one thing, our magazines are very compartmentalised, if I may be excused an awkward word. Some publications deal mostly with the foreign missions, some are for priests and religious, some are pious and devotional, some strictly theological, some catechetical or social or pastoral, more than one is devoted to a single interest like the Charismatic Renewal or the Pioneer Movement. If any reasonable number of our magazines were rather alike, or dealt with the living of the Christian Way on a broad front, then there could more easily be some amalgamation. As it is they are all (each one) rather limited in their readership and aims. Not in itself a bad thing but it has contributed to the inordinate number of publications that we have.

There is a further problem. Some 99 per cent of our magazines are owned by the religious orders and congregations. They tend to carry the flag of their particular owners. They serve often as advertising copy, especially the missionary magazines. They help to attract vocations. They sometimes have a long tradition in print. All resulting in a great hesitancy on the part of superiors to join forces with others.

There is one particularly unfortunate result of this situation. More than one religious congregation produces a magazine and does it badly. They need vocations, they need to be seen, as it were, they need help financially, they want to keep in touch with their friends, but the end product is rather miserable; a poor production, a colourless, drab-looking magazine, no professionalism about it. Nothing much to say. It does the religious magazine apostolate no service. It does it harm. In the bright, attractive world of the linear media it does religion itself harm. If any religious family wants to keep in touch with its members and its friends (and that is very important) it would be far better done, for example, by a regular in-house letter. It is time to leave the public arena to the professionals.

Meanwhile the Religious Press Association works on. First and foremost, it regularly seeks to bring to the notice of people the religious press itself and its work. It draws attention to important statements and documents of the Church, indeed of anyone or any group working for a better world. It helps its members (through meetings and lectures) to identify important questions and challenges as they appear. It provides a platform, a structure, a focus, all of which, in our noisy media world today, are vitally important if voices are to be heard and notice taken. The Association has, finally, been of some practical help to its members with everyday problems like VAT, postage costs, distribution. In 1983 the Association hosted the World Congress of the International Catholic Union of the Press. The format and structure of that Congress has been recognised abroad as a model of its kind.

🐾 🐾 🐾

Like all interests and ventures today – political, economic, religious – the Church press also has its international structures and presence. Indeed the religious media are far better organised internationally than they are in their respective homelands. You have UNDA, the International Catholic Association of Radio and Television, with its headquarters in Brussels. You have OCIC, the International Catholic Organisation for Cinema and the Audio-visual, with its headquarters in Amsterdam. And then you have UCIP, the International Catholic Union of the Press, with its general secretariat in Geneva.

The largest union of journalists of the world, UCIP is involved exclusively with the written word: books, magazines, dailies, periodicals, news agencies, research into the science of journalism and the techniques of teaching it. The initials UCIP stand for Union Catholique International de la Presse. It retains its French title as a tribute to its origins in 1927, mainly in the person of the distinguished French priest and journalist Emile Gabel. The Religious Press Association of Ireland has been a member of UCIP since 1977.

The organisation and structures of UCIP are very simple. It has a World President elected every three years. The day-to-day work is done by a permanent office and staff in Geneva. The rank-and-file members are divided into federations and regions. You have six federations, one each of Catholic journalists, of dailies, of periodicals, of Catholic news agencies, of teachers and researchers in journalism and the International Federation of Church Press Associations – the one to which Ireland belongs.

All these in turn work, too, on a regional basis: Latin America, Africa, three Asian regions, Europe and North America.

The World President is helped in his task by the various 'directive organs'. You have the General Assembly which meets every three years. The Council meets every year. It is made up of the elected officers of each federation and region. The Bureau meets twice a year and is composed of the presidents of the federations and regions. The Bureau of UCIP is its permanent organ of consultation. I had the honour of being elected twice to the Presidency of the

Federation of Religious Press Associations and so was a member of the Bureau for six years.

What are the aims of UCIP? They are presented very carefully in the official statutes: to encourage the presence and support the activities of Catholics in the various sectors of the Press in all its forms; to promote the development of Catholic journalism in every country; to promote and defend the right to information and freedom of opinion; to encourage research in journalism; to support and co-ordinate the activities of its own members and, lastly, to represent Catholic journalism at the various international institutions and organisations, both governmental and non-governmental. UCIP, for example, has its own representative at the United Nations.

Finally, there is an important figure: the Ecclesiastical Adviser. He is a priest chosen by the Holy See to advise on matters of doctrine. Which might be a good place to mention that one of the very significant and hopeful things about UCIP is the preponderance among its members of lay people, men and women. The present Secretary General is, in fact, an Indian lay Catholic, Joseph Chittilappilly. My own successor in the Bureau was an American journalist, Barbara Bickwith. In Ireland we have hardly begun to involve lay people in the Church Press. Until we do we are making poor provision for the future.

🐜 🐜 🐜

How effective is an international body like UCIP? Has it really helped the Church Press very much anywhere? To begin with, one has to say that UCIP is about 60 per cent a talk shop. This is inevitable. Its members are very scattered, they meet infrequently, the cultures and conditions in which its journalists work are very varied. It takes a lot of talking together to get down to agreed action or even agreed purposes. It comes down in the end to the fact that little or nothing is done if the talking and sharing are not done first. Having said that, it can fairly be claimed that UCIP does 40 per cent good work, a small portion of it very good work.

First of all, UCIP has a special care for Third World journalists. The term 'Third World' seems to have outlived its time. We are now using the phrase 'the developing countries' and sometimes 'the poor South'. However, names cannot hide poverty, lack of expertise, lack of training. UCIP does a great deal to help here. It is well organised in Asia, Africa and South America. It conducts seminars, discussions and practical demonstrations in the field of journalism for Catholics there. It encourages and supports early attempts at parish papers, newsletters, magazines, reporting. It brings the Third World journalists to its international meetings and congresses, all of which are a learning experience. In particular, it offers most useful financial contacts in Europe and the US, which have been of great assistance to struggling printing-presses and ill-supported publishers in the poorer Churches of Asia and Africa.

Then you have what is perhaps UCIP's most imaginative venture: the Summer University. In the jargon of the trade this is called 'a media exposure programme'. In practice what it involves is this: every two out of three years a group of about twenty-five journalists are taken out of their own continent and given about six weeks' experience of another continent, its culture, its history, it political structures. There are lectures, tours, demonstrations. For example, in 1988 a group of young journalists (non-European) were brought to Europe and spent six weeks experiencing and learning there, in Fribourg (Switzerland), Lyon (France) and Rome. In 1990 an outside group were brought to the US and Canada and spent their time studying conditions of life in North America for about two months. In 1991 the Summer University was organised in Asia. It takes little thought to realise that this is an excellent form of education and augurs well indeed for the future of the Church Press everywhere.

Finally, UCIP has developed what is called 'The Network of Young Journalists'. It has over seven hundred members in eighty-one countries. The Network provides a structure for young journalists up to the age of thirty-five. It is a forum in which they can talk and reflect together on what they should or could do for the welfare of others. The Network organises get-togethers and seminars, very often at international level.

The Network does two things: it provides structure or network itself, something which has a great attraction for and an appeal to young people; they love getting together for even no reason at all! Secondly, it is a source of invitation and encouragement coming from the Church: a call to young people to join in the great apostolate of the written word. The failure of the Church and its leaders to do this anywhere else, in any other form, is a great reproach and shame. The Network publishes its own newsletter, *News and Views*, and has a general convention every three years.

* * *

I described some of the work of UCIP as being very good indeed. Which it is and vitally needed. In the world of the Church media, in fact in the whole world of the media, secular or sacred, very little thought, if any, is given to what the media themselves really should be about. What, for example, is the actual role or purpose of the print media in any form? There are not many answers to that question, and worse again, little interest in it. As a result you have a thought vacuum in which very unacceptable positions are being taken up.

Archbishop, now Cardinal Francis Stafford of Denver, addressing the Annual Convention of the Catholic Press Association of America in ? said that, partly due to the shift in secular journalism from simply informing the public to becoming agents of social change, the modern world has 'turned away from truth in an unprecedented way'. The secular press, he went on, disseminates a vulgar relativism. There is no truth, only opinion. Your opinion, my opinion. He quoted George Orwell who said that language exists to communicate truths but that language in the twentieth century 'has been corrupted by deliberate euphemism, ambiguity and dishonesty – especially political dishonesty – on a massive scale'.

Incidentally, the Archbishop highlighted one of the deadliest influences on the print media. He said 'over the last two decades the culture of the press, an institution dedicated to informing and educating the public, has generally been overwhelmed and absorbed by the culture of television, an institution focused on entertaining consumers for profit'.

In this very confused and unreflecting scene UCIP has raised a voice. It has produced a series of well-thought-out documents dealing with the philosophical and ethical problems facing journalists in our time. Two of these documents or statements should be of immediate interest to everyone concerned with what is happening in our media world, and concerned especially with the spreading of the Good News of the gospel. The first of these statements, *Professional Ethics of the Journalist*, speaks to the whole world of the written word; the second statement, *The Ten Principles of the Catholic Church Press* will be of immediate concern for the Churches.

Leaving aside the technical terms which one usually finds in official documents, UCIP's Statement on Ethics says, in simple language:

- The right to information, the right to know is a fundamental right of each individual, each community, each people. That information should be unbiased, precise and complete.

- Remembering this right, the journalist must respect and promote it. As far as possible the journalist should use diverse sources of information, he or she must verify the facts and – very important – give a description of the context in which the facts are found.

- Information is to be understood as a social good, not as a commodity. Journalists are responsible for the information they transmit, responsible not only to the publisher but also to the public.

- The social role of the journalist demands that each acts in freedom and in accordance with their clear conscience. Journalists must refrain from disclosing sources of information or from receiving any form of illicit remuneration, direct or indirect. Journalists must resist excessive pressure from any source, whatever it may be.

- Journalists must be part of a dialogue with the public. They should promote participation by the public in the media. This means they must accept the public's right to correct, to rectify and to reply.

- A respect for the rights of the individual to privacy and human dignity demands from the journalist that they protect the reputation of others; all of which prohibits calumny, defamation, slander and insinuation.

- Journalists must respect the national community and its lawful institutions. The authorities, on their side, must protect the right to information and the inter-communication of its citizens; all of which provides a true public opinion and an authentic democracy.

• The journalist must defend religious freedom. He or she must respect the distinctive character and value of each culture, as well as the right of each people freely to choose their own destiny. The journalist must refuse all complicity in acts against life, or against the rights of ethnic groups, indeed against the survival of any group of human beings.

• Finally, journalists must be part of the struggle against the great evils of our time: poverty, disease, racism, illiteracy as well as aggressive war, the arms race and the regimes of tyranny.

* * *

Nobody can possibly read a thoughtful, balanced statement on ethics in journalism, such as that presented by UCIP, and not begin to think about, even be disconcerted (to say the least) by what is actually happening in the media of today. The problems begin with the very act of commenting: any adverse criticism at all of the world of journalism immediately becomes 'media bashing', and one has to add in fairness (remembering that other great institution in our everyday lives, the Church) that any adverse criticism of things ecclesiastical just as swiftly becomes 'Church bashing'.

These exchanges, as one knows over the years, are very futile. Is it possible, one wonders, to present the ideal picture of what might be in the written media – bearing in mind the principles we have been talking about – and in presenting that picture pass fair judgment, for those who have ears to hear, on what is going on around us.

Some points, however, have to be made. If the information offered by journalists must be 'unbiased, precise and complete', then journalists must give serious thought to the dangers of being, or being made to be, agents of social change.

Agents of social change will push their own positions, play down, perhaps misrepresent, those of other views, fail to give the full picture all round, pass at least implicit judgments, indulge in special pleading, be selective on a wide scale. Selectivity, incidentally, is modern journalism's besetting sin. One small point on sexuality referred to in a Church document will be the only point mentioned in the papers. If the document has no reference to sex at all, there is a good chance that the public won't hear, in the secular papers, anything at all of that document. One often wonders at how the sexual failures of public figures get wide billing but a seriously debilitating weakness like alcoholism will never be mentioned. That is selectivity.

If the journalist must use diverse sources of information, verify the facts and – vitally – describe the context in which they are found, then the journalist must work hard. It can't be done sitting at a desk, ringing around (and sometimes mushrooming what has been said), picking the brains of somebody who has done a little work on the subject or raiding another's work and then claiming the slovenly result to be a balanced report. On the point of context, we might do well to send all sub-editors on a short course dealing with the meaning of context and especially the implications of it. Some of our headlines and shoulder-headings might, as a result, be a little less pathetic, certainly less misleading.

🐜 🐜 🐜

Information, according to our principles, is not a commodity. It is not to be managed and packaged. We cannot treat that bit of information which sells papers as paramount and play down or ignore the rest. If we do, we are on our way to sensationalism, sleaze, even pornography, to very poor journalism, to say the least.

If the public have a right 'to correct, to rectify and to reply', then journalists must, again, take that right seriously. It is not taken seriously when letters and protests are rubbished, even ignored, when people replying are labelled and pigeon-holed, described as 'right-wing', 'controversial', 'predictable', 'well-known members' of this or that. Justice and fairness have never been easy virtues but they are vital ingredients in building that world which journalists so often claim to want: a more liberal, decent and caring society.

One of the most difficult areas in which to see one's way (in the world of the media) is that of the individual's right to privacy.

How much privacy has one a right to who has, by office or deliberate design, become a very public figure? When are facts about the private lives of such people 'matters of public interest'? To what extent does unacceptable behaviour in private affect the duties and capabilities of public figures? It is not always easy to answer these questions completely but if one bears in mind humane principles like those of UCIP, one comes near doing as little harm as possible: don't trade in lies or half-truths; don't touch the personal reputation of anyone if it has nothing to do with the facts in discussion; don't insinuate or hint at anything which might, unnecessarily, be to the discredit of persons involved; never forget that each of us has a dignity and a whole web of feeling which demand of everyone else respect and reverence.

And one might add: when a person is down, when their reputation is gone, when journalists can with impunity before the law say what they like about him or her – in that moment let each of us who has ever taken a pen or touched a typewriter remember a fellow human being in need and not trample a soul in the dust. If we do, we dishonour ourselves, bring a great profession into disrepute, and inflict a wound on journalism from which it does not deserve to recover.

♣ ♣ ♣

Then there is the second thoughtful document to come from UCIP: *The Ten Principles of the Catholic Church Press.* These principles have to do with the role of the written word in the preaching of the gospel, in helping the people live their faith in our kind of world.

The document begins with a sentence taken directly from the Church's best document this century on the role and meaning of the mass media (*Communio et progressio,* 1972). It reads: 'At one and the same time the Church Press will be a mirror which reflects the world and a light to show the world the way.' Simply, it is not the role of the Church Press merely to indulge in pieties, very particularly not to indulge in endless, useless trivia, in what Von Hugel called 'village pump and parish drain', but to present our world as it is, sins and all. And so present it as to help Christians understand our times and see, in the light of their beliefs, how best to deal with our age and change it, if we must. Nobody denies that it is the obvious duty of the Church Press to present the teachings of the Church and the ideals of the Christian message but many Christians, especially Catholics, take offence when they find in Church publications what they would regard as unsavoury; forgetting the very point of Christ's coming, to say nothing of his death upon the cross. As St John put it: 'You know very well my friends that when he was revealed to us it was to take away our sins.' The Church Press is part of that task. It has to face sin. It is a fallen, broken world which we are trying to mend.

* * *

The Ten Principles then go on to stress a point of pressing urgency: the financial support of the Church Press. The document demands that the Church Press be furnished 'with *as much of the necessary personnel and resources as the Church supplies to her other activities* in the pastoral and educational fields'. To her reproach this has not been done by the Church. (How many times have any of us ever seen a collection taken up for the Church media?) Pope John Paul said in 1991 in *Redemptoris Missio:* 'Generally speaking, preference has been given to other means of preaching the Gospel and of Christian education while the mass media are left to the initiative of individuals or small groups and enter into pastoral planning only in a secondary way.'

For 'small groups' read, in the Irish context, the religious orders and congregations who carry the lion's share of the challenge. Even more recently, the official Church pressed the point again: 'The great contemporary Areopagus of the mass media has more or less been neglected by the Church' (*Aetatis Novae*, 1992). All this has to be said and we only make a start when we recognise it.

One vital form of Church support for the written media, of course, is help towards the training and preparation of editorial staff. We educate and prepare people for every role in life today, not just in the Church but across all the professions and avocations, but expect editors and producers of religious papers and magazines to come fully armed out of the air. Some small steps have been taken in this direction but we have most of the way to go yet. It takes a great deal of professionalism and training to be able to help people, through the media, negotiate our world today in the light of Christian principles and help our world reflect on itself with the assistance of that same faith. This is at the heart of the task.

* * *

'The Catholic Church Press must report fully, truly, accurately and openly. In doing so it meets the right of every believer to be able to inform himself or herself about everything which our active participation in the life of the Church demands.' This principle, in our document, reflects very strongly our kind of world but it is not an easy road to follow.

The Church is a family, it has great pride in itself, and it is very deeply hurt when abuses and scandals come into the open. Like any household it wants to keep the problems 'in the family'. But can the problems be solved that way? Some aspects of justice demand that things come out in public, that admissions and clarifications and amends be made, that guilty people be identified, that steps be taken, and be seen to be taken, that wrong and sinful deeds do not happen again.

On the other hand, the Church, very especially the Catholic Church, has its enemies. They have been dancing on what they thought was her grave for almost two thousand years. With any kind of historical sense at all one wonders: will they never learn? But they are there and ready to use every abuse and failing in the Church to discredit religion. It does not make for an easy response to demands of visibility and openness. These demands of justice and truth, however, must be met. It is, perhaps, a good example of the healthy tension: on the one hand openness and justice must be served and at the same time the basic good name and good cause of the Church must not be irreparably damaged.

* * *

Ronald Rolheiser is a distinguished Church Press columnist in North America. He offers a very good example, in his writing, of the Church Press facing up to moral problems in the Church while, at the same time, setting the correct perspective and righting the balance.

Take one scene: he is talking about the United States and Canada. There is, he says, an extremely simplistic and erroneous identification being made today in the world and in the Church. When you say the word 'paedophilia' people automatically think of 'priest'. They then compound this misjudgment by making another connection: celibacy, lack of sex. Celibates don't have sex, as married people do, and so are obviously susceptible to this kind of thing.

He goes on to demonstrate how the facts so belie all this that one has to wonder if the common acceptance by people is just simple ignorance or the product of real malice.

First of all, less than one per cent (in fact a small fraction of one per cent) of all paedophilia and sexual abuse is perpetrated by priests and other consecrated religious; which in no way, of course, excuses those sad and shameful people. Statistically, sexual abuse of children happens in one out of every three to four houses on every street in North America. Given the magnitude of the tragedy one can only ask why the issue is so concentrated around less than one per cent of the guilty?

Secondly, paedophilia, he points out, has no significant relationship to celibacy. It is an indiscriminate disease. It makes no difference whether one is married or not, whether one has lots of sex or no sex at all. It is indeed ironic that consecrated celibates are proportionately less likely to be paedophiles than other people. This fact is rarely brought to the fore. It is the role and duty of the Church Press – papers and magazines – to do so.

Rolheiser concludes with balance: 'Where is the justice in tarring all priests and religious with the stigma of paedophilia when the vast majority of them are totally innocent? But injustice to priests and religious is, in the end, not the biggest danger here. As priests and religious we do, in fact, deserve some brutal challenges to clean up our act. One instance of sexual abuse is one instance too many. It is time some veins were bled. Hence some of the rage directed against us will do us good!'

* * *

There is an old amusing story of the pious Victorian parson saying his prayers. He began: 'Dear Lord, as no doubt you have seen already in this morning's *Times*...'. But the story has a point. There is no idea more pressed on us in recent years, no work with which we are more familiar than that of 'dialogue'. Dialogue is a converse, a conversation, a listening, an exchange of ideas by which we develop our thinking, and learn the way forward for all of us together.

But where is this dialogue to take place? The parson put it, presumably, on the letters page of the London *Times*! No bad place. In fact, today, the mass media provide about the only forum for dialogue and exchange among people, very particularly and at its best, the linear medium: papers and journals.

The document that we are talking about here (*The Ten Principles*), puts as one of the main functions of the Catholic Press the provision of a forum of genuine dialogue within the Church, reflecting both the Church's unity and diversity. It must also provide a forum for dialogue between the Church and the wider world.

There is no life in the Church without dialogue, no decent public opinion, no richness in prayer. There is no experience of the Holy Spirit working in the Church and the world unless we are encouraged to talk together, to listen, exchange, hear the Spirit who speaks in each of us, sometimes perhaps very distantly. The poet Neruda reflected: 'So that you can hear Me at times my words get fainter and fainter, like the marks made by seagulls on the sand.'

All this is closely tied in to the tension which we talked about between being open and honest on the one hand, while respecting the Church's sometimes delicate positions on the other. But the fact remains: there must be questions and protests and opinions expressed and listening done in any worthwhile Church Press venture. We cannot, for example, be selective (and we have been) towards Vatican II. We cannot over-concentrate on *Lumen gentium*, on the faithful concurring in the teaching of the bishops with religious submission, on showing obedience in a special way to the authentic magisterium of the Roman Pontiff – and forget *Gaudium et spes* which tells us that the Church does not always have a ready answer to particular questions, that all the faithful have just the same freedom of enquiry, of thought, of humble and courageous expression in those matters about which they know something.

Even common sense tells us that unless we are open, articulate and humane in the living of the Church's life we will not help the Church much to adjust to our world, or have anything very much to say to it.

* * *

How does all this work out in practice, specifically in the Church Press around us? Very fitfully, one would have to say. I was editor of *Reality* magazine for eighteen years and closely involved with the Religious Press Association during that time. I enjoyed every moment of it, frustrating, even maddening, though it was at times.

The fundamental problem was, I believe, a lack of reflection and of thought on our own part. Over the years we did not give enough consideration (if any) to a 'reading' of the situation, of the signs of the times. In the context of the Irish Church and its mission we are a nation in reaction. The Church's role in the past was immense, through the dark days and into freedom.

The influence of Catholic teaching reached into our Constitution, the making of our laws, education, health, social services, even recreation. We are now reacting against this – inevitably. This reaction, interestingly, can be seen very clearly in a comparison: our media's mild treatment of minorities, religious or secular, and the very different story when it comes to the great looming presence of the Catholic Church.

Therefore, we have to read the so-called 'attack' on the Church correctly. Merely accepting and 'living with' the media in Ireland as 'hostile to the Church – period' is not very helpful. If we are talking about a reaction, and we are, then the very first step to take is to accept the fact and find in it the truth and justice which are surely there. It is so with all reactions.

The next direction we have to take – and do not always – is to be sensitive in the way we preach, teach and write. Condemnation and denunciation are especially unsuited to our time. They tend to affirm people's views that the Church is backward-looking, closed, even dismissive.

This is not easy. Speaking a few years ago (1986) at a Conference of the International Federation of Church Press Associations in Spain, I said: 'Once we have made a plea with the Church and its media for compassion and understanding, we are immediately faced with an extraordinary and delicate task: how to be compassionate and Christ-like and, at the same time, not take the wrong stand or refuse to take the hard stand when the Church and its mission offer no other choice. This is at the very centre of the challenge facing the Church media in Ireland today; it faces the Church media everywhere.'

These words grew out of my experience in our Church Press here. We simply did not recognise that there was a delicate task to hand, that there was a tension to hold between compassion and straight talk, that it needed a great deal of openness and reflection – and training. We opted so often instead (in our popular Church publications) for the photos, the past, the well-trodden facts, the obvious, and now and then the broadside on some issue or other. Or worse, rode in with the popular media, with the fads and fashions, to get attention.

This, of course, is not remotely true of every Church publication in Ireland. Some have carried banners bravely for many a day. Some have fondly remembered (as I do personally) the vision and the hope of a giant among us, the late Canon Gerry McGarry, the founder of *The Furrow*.

Then there is the search for, and the acknowledgement we must make of the real and positive values in modern liberal stances. Bishop Donal Murray wrote recently: 'Many people, including many good Catholics, may be unnecessarily alienated if these new currents [liberalism, feminism, pluralism] are approached in terms of mere condemnation rather than as cultural realities to be deepened, enlightened and, where necessary, purified in the light of the Gospel.' We did not, do not always have this positive approach in our religious publications, and their general ineffectiveness is one of the sad results.

Then again, we have our extremists. For want of better labels (but readily understood) the right wing, conservatives, and the left wing, liberals. When it comes to ignorance, silliness and obnoxiousness the right wins hands down. Not only have they little idea of what theology is about or even any idea of what Church history teaches but they are self-appointed guardians of the faith, as they know it, with the result that they are closed, dismissive and damaging to an extraordinary degree.

On the other side you have the left. They are a mixed bag ranging from the atheistic to those who never even give religion a thought. Some are positively anti-Christian, actually regarding religion as a force for ignorance and backwardness. Some are anti-clerical, mostly of the pub-talk variety. We do not have in Ireland the poisonous political anti-clericalism of, say, Spain or France. The Catholic Church has been too deeply identified with the national struggle for far too long for that. Which is not to say that there is not a good deal of adverse criticism of the clergy. There is and increasingly so.

But this has to be said about the so-called liberals, the left wing. They don't have closed minds, rather part of their problem is their minds are too open! You can argue with them, discuss, have some mutual listening. You cannot do this with the right wing. Not that these so-called conservatives are always wrong. They are sometimes right. But they are so self-righteous and off-putting that one tends to flee. As George Bernard Shaw put it: part of the problem about being right is the people you find yourself with!

I am talking here about extreme or radical right and left. There are in Ireland, as everywhere, many good Christians; they know their faith and their history but are very concerned about the future and the insistent undermining of the values and traditions which are vital for the future of all of us. They want to preserve what is best from the past and hold the roots firm in a very confused time. They do honour to the name of 'conservative'.

There are, as well, many excellent but different kinds of people concerned about the Church and the faith. They have travelled and read widely but feel deep down that we are, as a Church, very inward-looking, constricted, even fearful. They would hope that the Church were open, more trusting, less paternalistic, more humane. These are very important people in the life of the Church. They, in their turn, do honour to the name 'liberal'.

* * *

The normal channel through which authority in the Church works is that of superiors, in practice, in the broad public arena, the bishops. Not only is it part of today's fashion to attack the bishops but, in true Irish style, we get hung up on a half-humorous, half-mythical phrase like 'the belt of a crozier'. Our thinking on the subject tends to stop there.

In my eighteen years editing a popular magazine, well-known to the bishops and certainly read by some of them, I never experienced anything except courtesy and kindness. There were difficulties, especially in areas like moral theology. One had to be 'careful' – as indeed the bishops themselves had. Moral theology (the guidelines on right and wrong) has never been a field in which anyone can be all that certain about anything. One of the greatest moral theologians in the history of the Church, St Alphonsus, said that moral theology was a morass and always would be.

There were, and are, areas in which one would be adversely critical of Church leadership in the world, certainly in the area of the written word. Something of the bishops' suspicion and fear *vis-à-vis* the secular media was very easily able to affect Church publications too. We could all, at times, be branded by what has almost come to be a pejorative word: the media.

Again there is that failing – and it is right across the whole face of the Christian experience – a lack of trust in each other. Bishops often don't trust the people enough and more than one of them has said so. But, then, people don't always trust the bishops either. In a recent study by Donald Nicholl of the role of the Catholic hierarchy during the Hitler nightmare in Germany, the author comes to some fascinating conclusions. One of them is that the bishops failed to trust the ordinary Catholic people to ride out the storm. They failed to trust them, he stresses, out of real concern for and love of their people. They were anxious to protect them, they went along with a great deal of so-called Nazi philosophy so as not to burden the people with more than they might bear. Had they left them to their best selves or pointed the way to the mountain (as on one occasion they were certainly asked to do) things could have been different. It is easy for us now, after the event, to be wise and high-minded, but at least let us learn the lessons. It is best put in the good old journalistic line: 'Give light and the people will find their own way.'

In general, one has to say that we Catholics are over-critical of each other: the Pope, bishops, priests, laity. There are mixed-up reasons for this but it is at least important to say so. Sometimes it strikes one suddenly – in the confessional, in counselling, in crises – how marvellous and good people are. Anyone who has ever conducted a priests' retreat must be driven to the reflection: what a dedicated, concerned and good body of men they are. Nor can that comment be confined to the clergy. In the early 1970s there was a very moving book written by a non-Catholic called *The R.C.s.* In it the author, George Scott, said: 'Among the clergy and among the ordinary men and women of the Church, I encountered a religious zeal, a scrupulosity in personal conduct and a goodness and love in personal living on a scale I have never know before.'

♠ ♠ ♠

Has the Church Press – papers, magazines, periodicals – got a future? Or do we need it? Serious doubts might be raised in answering the first question. No doubt at all in answering the second: we certainly do need the Church Press.

Reading itself is the first hurdle. It demands, as so often

stressed, time, patience, reflection, effort; but we are today the people of the ready fix, the instant result, the painless road. Gadgetry and technology, which claim an easy way to information and knowledge, have an infinite attraction for us: VCRs, CD-Roms, modems, computers, interactive cable. Even a hundred years ago Emerson could say 'things are in the saddle and ride mankind'.

In passing, it is worth noticing that one of the most extraordinary facts about our modern media revolution is that it has not increased human knowledge at all. The Times Mirror company has polled young adults (in the US) for many years. Since the mid-1970s this age-group has shown a steady decrease in knowledge about the great issues and news events of our time. Americans today, for example, are less aware of the world and more self-absorbed than they were thirty years ago. And all against the background of an explosion in communications technology beyond our dreams. One is reminded again of Ralph W. Emerson. When told that the telephone enabled Maine to speak to Florida, he asked: 'But has Maine anything to say to Florida?'

The problem actually goes deeper. Addressing a group of Catholic journalists when Archbishop Stafford of Denver said: 'Consider this one item. It speaks volumes about our inability to find beauty, radiant goodness or truth in the real world. For the first time ever, reported this year, more university level students are preparing for a career in public relations than in journalism. It is more satisfying in the minds of young people today to put the right spin on reality than merely to report it.'

The second hurdle we face on our way to save the day for reading is television: its great looming presence, gulping down all our interest, attention and time.

Should we forget about the written word in the spreading of the Good News and leave the field to TV? Let it do the teaching, the instructing, the teasing out of ideas, the turning over of concepts, the intellectual challenging, the balancing, the thousand things which are part of communicating the faith and helping us all think and grow and live as children of God.

But TV cannot do this, or at least very little of it. A book published a short time ago in the US has rightly received wide attention: *Amusing Ourselves To Death* by Neil Postman. In it he raises the vital issue of TV's tendency to make everything – politics, policy, education, religion – into entertainment: the brief slot, the passing image, the amusing 'bite', the next item. The phrase 'serious TV' is a contradiction in terms – mostly.

We, of previous generations, have come from the age of exposition, of exploration, the world of print which helped people to think, which valued order and logic, which allowed for the delayed response, gave room for reflection and thought. We are now, thanks to television, in the age of show-business. Show-business is all about entertainment, glitz, movement, the passing lights, no concentration on anything. Show-business, which is more and more today's TV, is obviously unable to take the place of the printed word in the spreading of the Gospel. Add to the world of TV the money, the profit motive, and you get a medium which gives to people what they want, not what they need. Which is not, of course, remotely the way in preaching the faith.

These comments may be based very much on the US television scene. But let us have no doubt about it, it is all coming our way soon (as some of our own Irish TV already demonstrates). The experience which has created 'a generation of visually oriented Americans with the attention span of a flash bulb' will wash over us all in the end.

There can be no doubting, on the other hand, the marvellous service which the printed word offers in the spreading and the receiving of the Good News. It offers us, first and foremost, 'room' and time. We can come back, again and again, to what has been written, think over it, read it again, see more in it, understand. In the famous phrase: *scripta manent*, the written words remain. The words and images of TV and radio and even telephone are gone as soon as they come. As Garrison Keillor put it: 'There are no neatly wrapped packages of phone calls in the attic to remind us of what has been said.'

And we need that 'room' and space for more than one reason. Many concepts, for example, conscience, sacrament, even God, need to be explained, put in different ways, eased into our understanding. It is only in the quiet and peaceful reading among the depths and reaches of our faith that we can really learn and grow. We have always, in fact, to be going back to the word on the page. No wonder that the world's three great faiths are all founded on a book.

Sometimes it strikes me how ill-equipped many Christians are *vis-à-vis* their faith. You meet good people, professional people, well-informed and mature in all the secular areas of their living, but they are children when it comes to a knowledge of the faith or any ability to give an account of it. Why? Because they do not read. Anyone who thinks that listening every Sunday to a homily (even supposing it is a good one!) is sufficient to feed the mind and heart in the face of our bleak world is not doing a lot of thinking. And soon even the Sunday homily may be gone as people give up going to Mass. Then the Church Press must come into its own. In fact, in Germany more people read the Church Press than attend church. Does it have to come to this before we will listen?

In defending the Church Press, in promoting it, I feel so strongly that it is the obvious thing to do and say. Yet apparently not, it is all so uphill. But how can we be informed if we do no reading! How can we defend the Faith, even to ourselves, if we do no reflecting on it, find no clarification anywhere, hear nobody else negotiate its mysteries? How can we pray if our minds and hearts are empty of stimulation or questions? How can we relate a two-thousand-year-old message to our mixed-up times without the help of people who are at least skilled enough to say something, sometimes, which helps or enlightens?

We are, in fact, all guilty – priests and people – of not giving good literature, often simple Catholic literature, the place it should have in Christian lives. Speaking of priests, C. S. Lewis has a fascinating fact: the hardest thing to believe, he says, is that which you have just explained or defended to somebody else. When you pour yourself out you become hollow inside. The priest is warned: unless he can regularly refresh his inner self with quiet times of prayer and reading he will begin to doubt those very things which he holds most dear.

But, we do not lose hope. There is something about the Church Press, indeed about all literature, serious or popular, dealing with the Lord and his Spirit among us, which tells us it will endure. Even the extraordinary sense of buoyancy and hope which one finds among those who work in the Religious Press has its own message. I know of no one who worked with me in this apostolate over the years who would doubt its future or fail to believe that in the years to come it will, if possible, be more necessary than ever: for our enemies will have their pens too. As G. K. Chesterton put it in his great poem 'The Ballad of the White Horse':

> *I have a vision and I know*
> *The heathen shall return.*
> *They shall not come with warships,*
> *They shall not waste with brands*
> *But books be all their eating*
> *And ink be on their hands.*

ȧ ȧ ȧ

In 1970 the Irish Episcopal Conference founded *Intercom,* a monthly magazine designed to serve the pastoral needs of clergy and religious in Ireland. Nearly thirty years later *Intercom* is still to the good, having passed through both the good and the bad times.

I was invited to become editor in November 1994, and the first issue of 1995 (February) was my starting-post. My last issue was the December/January 1997/98 number. I had a simple brief. I was to edit a magazine principally directed at priests and religious, keeping happily in mind the fact that it was gradually reaching a wider audience. The purpose of the magazine was to help readers in their professional and spiritual needs, to highlight good works and initiatives in the Church, to encourage and support those who serve in the many (especially liturgical) ministries, to be a signpost of hope. It was in part, I believe, to be about morale. It was never to be an angry broadsheet (or broadside!), in spite of all the pressures in that direction from certain sources.

It was, however, around this very point of the magazine's purpose and policy that the controversy erupted when I took over from my predecessor, Fr Kevin Hegarty. One side saw *Intercom*'s role and function as I have just described it. The other side saw *Intercom* as a debating forum, as a voice of change and challenge – among other things. But, considering that *Intercom* was a publication of the Catholic Communications Institute under the aegis of the Bishops' Commission, it does not take a lot of foresight to see trouble down the road were the magazine to become angry, hyper-critical of Church or Church positions, ill at ease with traditional stances, rattling and shaking structures long wished by some to be gone. I am not for a moment saying that such was *Intercom* under Kevin Hegarty. What I am saying (a little colourfully perhaps) is that the editor's role was and is a very sensitive one and trouble could quickly blow up considering where *Intercom* was coming from and in whose house it dwelt.

At the time I took over the Editor's chair there was a lot of anger. That was understandable. What was not so acceptable was the offensiveness and the insensitivity of some people (whose training should have helped) towards the new editor – especially in the form of rowing in with the secular media which were singularly uninformed and predictable in the whole event.

There is one comment from the controversy which has stayed with me. Somewhere along the line in the protests and letters (new Editor v old Editor etc.) the claim was made that *Intercom* had been on the way to becoming an 'Irish *Tablet*'. Now I would yield to none in a knowledge of the famous London *Tablet*. I have read it consistently over forty years and with countless others (not just across English-speaking lands) regard it as the best journal of its kind in the world. *Intercom* never came remotely near it – never, I suspect, aimed to – is not remotely like it now and never will be. Perhaps this *Tablet* reference encapsulates (certainly throws an interesting light on) all the nonsense and phoniness which to such an unpleasant extent marked the change of editor in 1995.

I should in all this have to pay personal tribute to my predecessor Fr Kevin Hegarty. In his handing over to me he treated me with great courtesy and kindness, painful though I'm sure it was for himself. I am grateful to him.

* * *

I have used one word repeatedly in referring to our secular press: predictable. In his book *Media In Ireland: the Search For*

Diversity, the editor Damien Kiberd wrote: 'I have worked as a journalist for 17 years. One thing I found most remarkable about the world of Dublin journalism is the relative absence of internal debate. Journalists tend to travel in packs. Like the peloton following the man in the yellow jersey during the Tour de France, the corps of journalists based at RTE and with the national newspapers tends to adopt uniform opinions upon the issues of the day. As the necessity to research facts by contacting members of the wider public evaporates... the possibility that the peloton might be wholly out of touch with public opinion can, at times, reach dangerous proportions.... To put it plainly, instead of talking to ordinary people, many journalists may actually spend a large part of the day talking to each other.'

In that same volume Professor Joe Lee writes: 'Look at the opinion columns of the newspapers. A handful of commentators are worth reading because they are sufficiently unpredictable to be interesting.... But in most cases you can press a button and know what you are going to get before the content comes out.'

The most specifically serious charge made, certainly against the broadcast media, is in the context of its public service role. Again Professor Lee writes: 'RTÉ authorities would strenuously deny that there was an RTÉ line on (for example) no-fault divorce. And they would be right. There was no RTÉ line. There didn't have to be. Programme makers had so internalised a value system conducive to no-fault divorce that there was a *de facto* line, even while *de jure* the stance of the station was no doubt correct. That is the most effective type of line of all.'

In other words, we may talk about and claim (for our media) openness, balance, access, pluralism, but that talk means little if the actual custodians of the airwaves or the print lines are themselves suspect or have sold the pass. The old classic phrase keeps haunting the human story: 'Quis custodiet ipsos custodes?' Who will watch the watchers?

🐾 🐾 🐾

I have been asked what it is like to edit a publication aimed mainly at priests and religious. 'Rather daunting, I should have thought', suggested one innocent questioner. Not in the least – and not because the editor has any special graces or accomplishments, but rather because of the clerical readership itself. Priests, like most people today, do not, in the main, do much reading, or are not much interested in literature of any kind.

There is, I think, a particularly large lethargy today surrounding the written word and its aims or uses. One would have thought, for example, after all the controversy three years ago surrounding the departure of Fr Kevin Hegarty which raised so many questions about the role and content of *Intercom,* that, when the readers of the magazine got their chance in 1996 in a professional 'questionnaire' survey, they would have made their voices heard. Not at all. The response was 4.2 per cent. In plain figures, 195 readers responded to 7,000 questionnaires!

* * *

One particular objection to my editorial policy would come in every now and then. It was a complaint against reprinting articles from other sources. It always puzzled me. I have been a fairly omnivorous reader and keep my eye on articles and essays appearing across a fairly wide spectrum of publications.

This is particularly easy to do, when one lives in a theological and pastoral centre. There is a great monthly influx of magazines and journals. When one comes on a good piece, why not reprint it if it is worth it? The readers of *Intercom,* for example, certainly the vast majority of them, would not have had a chance to see the original themselves and might perhaps need to read it. Why try to get somebody to do a similar piece if it is already done and well done? But the tendency to re-invent the wheel is deep in all human nature!

Another small but important point in this connection: it is far more troublesome and time-consuming to republish articles than to publish new original ones. With the latter you just commission, receive, and either publish or not. With reprints you have to get permission from the author, from the publisher of the journal, sometimes from its editor – with changes and cuts submitted and cleared, all involving phone calls, faxes, letters, refusals. If an editor wants a quiet life, he should forget about reprinting. And yet the complaints came. Some people just don't recognise when they are being done a favour or service.

* * *

A few years ago, the well-know Peruvian priest and theologian Gustavo Gutierrez visited Ireland. After he had spoken to the Religious Press Association, I asked him how he would preach Liberation Theology (he is often credited with being its founder) to the people at Mass in Rathgar on the up-coming Sunday. He replied that he would not be able to preach the Good News to the people of Rathgar because he did not know them. You can only preach the gospel, he said, when you are at one with your audience, are in step with 'the pace and tempo' of their time and place.

This incident came to me many times during the drawn-out exchanges which I, as editor, had with readers of *Intercom* on the subject of the Prayers of the Faithful. I was against *Intercom* supplying, every Sunday, ready-made, ready-to-pour prayers for the priest to use each week. In the March 1997 issue, Fr Paddy Jones, Director of the National Centre for Liturgy, wrote: 'Pre-packaged prayers now published in a variety of journals and books (and some looking even better than the liturgical books) have limited value. It is much better to try and formulate the intercessions for which a particular congregation should pray.'

The General Intercessions were restored to the Church's liturgy following the Vatican II Constitution of 1963. They did indeed have, in part, a general and fixed format following the ancient directive of 1 Timothy 2:4: 'I urge that petitions, prayers, intercessions and thanksgivings be offered for all peoples, for sovereigns and all in high office that they may lead a quiet and tranquil life, in full observance of religion, and high standards of morality. Such prayer is right and approved by God our Saviour, whose will is that all should be saved and come to know the truth.'

But the Prayers of the Faithful, while having in part a fixed format, were also meant to be (mostly, I should think) a very real part in the ongoing struggle for help and a lived faith in any given parish or community. The General Instruction of the Roman Missal (45-47) directs the sequence of intentions to be:

a. for the needs of the Church
b. for public authorities and the salvation of all
c. for those oppressed by any need
d. for the local community

All told, I think we have done little reflection on the Prayers of the Faithful, with the result that they have been

weakened and stylised, have been shunted into rote and
routine forms, have lost their impact. For example, we have
confused *intentions* with prayer. Intentions are not prayers,
nor are they addressed to God. We have mixed up *petition* and
thanksgiving. What on earth is the meaning of a rigmarole like
'We thank you Lord for giving us a lovely new body... Lord
hear us, Lord graciously hear us!' One is even surprised at how
few priests, even on weekdays, will offer a petition prompted
by the Word just read. And sometimes that petition can throw
a new light on the very Word just spoken. Let's hope things
improve.... Lord hear us!

🐵 🐵 🐵

Has *Intercom* a future? Should it have one? I believe it should.
Let me put it this way: I am reading, as I write, an excellent
book on the Priesthood, entitled *New Hearts For New Models:
A Spirituality for Priests Today* by Daniel J. O'Leary (Columba
Press, Dublin). The author reflects: 'The priest, as the weaver
of wholeness, is the one who hears and transcribes the music
of what happens. He is the one who puts together ... the
fragments and splinters, of a desperately disoriented sequence
of lived experiences.... The huge issues of universal freedom
for people to live and worship according to their beliefs, to
have equal rights and privileges in society, to live in an
environment of peace and justice, to break through what Pope
John Paul calls "the culture of death" into a "civilisation of
love" [all this] must be addressed by the priest weaver.'

In more prosaic language, the priest should make sense of
things for the rest of us, sense in our confused, argumentative
and sometimes miserable world. All around us are the
conflicting forces of secularism, consumerism, hedonism,

individualism, fanaticism – as well as goodness, heroism and the faith. How give directions? How find a meaning today? How weave the wholeness? Who is better placed to help than the priest, considering his vocation and the reasons why he answered the call? That call was, and is, a call to follow in a special way, and show forth the One who is the Way, the Truth and the Life; the One who is the supreme Weaver of Wholeness.

With this large canvas in mind, one can begin to see a role for *Intercom* – in a smaller picture, of course. Since Vatican II we have been deluged with books, articles, lectures, papers, seminars on renewal and change. In our Irish Church Press scene alone we face a flood of magazines: liturgical, pastoral, catechetical, historical, moral, to say nothing of a Niagara of information on a new sociology and a new theology of the religious life. Who can read all this, even a fraction of it? Who can make sense of it? We certainly need a weaver of wholeness!

Intercom could help. It could help sort out, condense, recommend, reject, explain, suggest – all in this vast world of the written medium and in a way that might help us negotiate and take in at least some of what has been said or written, good and bad. There have been attempts to do this in the form, for example, of theological digests. They have not always been successful, but we can always try again. *Intercom* is there, a ready instrument, as it were, to this purpose, in part at least!

And one thing I am sure of: were *Intercom* killed off in the morning one would have by evening a suggestion that we should have a magazine to do such a service! Who said the Lord, in creating us, did not have a sense of humour!

At first sight the title of the book is strange. It is *The Stature of Waiting* by W. H. Vanstone. If you have read the book, I need say little; if you have not, I hardly know where to begin. But I do know that of all the books I have ever read, this is the one which will come back to me in the end. At least, I hope it will.

With profound apologies and thanks to the author, let me follow one of its themes – always hoping that I am within earshot of the book's message.

There is a famous and indelible scene in the New Testament. It is in all four Gospels: the betrayal of Christ by Judas. The scene is immortalised by Caravaggio in his great masterpiece *The Taking of Christ* and is sometimes described by Scripture scholars as 'the Handing Over'. (Professor William Klessen of the École Biblique claims that the word *sakar*, meaning 'the one handing over', is the root basis of the name Iskariot.)

Let's take two Gospels: St Mark (representing the Synoptics) and St John. To begin with Mark: in the first half of the Gospel Jesus is never the mere observer of a scene or one who waits on events. He took them up the mountain, he dismissed the Pharisees. He leaves behind him a trail of change: fishermen no longer at their nets, sick people restored to health, a girl raised from the dead, a storm calmed.

Even in quiet moments Jesus is in control. Take the calling of the twelve: he went up the mountain, he appointed twelve, he sent them forth. He gave new names to Peter and the Sons of Thunder. At Caesarea Philippi he came, he asked, he rebuked, he began to teach, he called the crowd. Mark reports scenes as Jesus sees them: he saw them casting their nets, he saw the Spirit descend, he saw Levi sitting at his desk, he found them asleep. To emphasise the activity of Jesus, Mark speaks of the inner workings of his mind: Jesus had compassion, he wondered at their disbelief, he knew power had gone out of him.

Then a remarkable change takes place, 'the handing over' takes place, the betrayal by Judas. Jesus is still the centre of the story, but he is no longer the actor, the initiator of events, no longer, as it were, the subject of the sentence. After the betrayal Mark reports not a single incident seen through the eyes of Jesus. Preachers may talk about the courage or patience of Jesus in his Passion but they don't learn that from St Mark. Even simple activities like 'going' or 'standing' or 'turning' are not so described. Always they took him, they led him, they dressed him. The very few times when Jesus speaks now, his words are disregarded as ineffectual or resigned. 'Do you come against me with staves? – let the Scriptures be fulfilled.' 'Are you the King of the Jews? – thou hast said it, have it your way.' Jesus is no longer the one in charge, the one who acts or orders. He is now the object of the verb, as it were. He is the one done to.

Let us now turn to St John's Gospel. There you have the very same pattern. After 'the handing over' you have a complete reversal of what went before. We notice this by keeping an eye on the phrase the 'works' of Jesus, the 'working' of Jesus. This word hardly appears in any of the other Gospels (once in Matthew and once in Luke) but between the third and seventeenth chapters of St John you have twenty-four references to the works of Jesus. And the working is always free. Many try to stop him or fetter him but they fail. Twice they attempt to stone him. There are six references in John to attempts to 'take' him but always 'nobody laid hands on him'. He passed out of their hands. The people of Jerusalem are surprised that one whom 'they are seeking to kill' is still able to speak 'freely'. John makes clear, however, that Jesus' time for work is limited; 'We must work, the works of him who sent me, while it is day'.

Then the change takes place, 'the handing over'. This change in the role and status of Jesus is clear in St Mark through his factual style and manner of writing. It is suggested in St John by a reversal of the ideas 'working', 'works', power freely exercised. At the Last Supper Jesus said 'I have finished the work thou gavest me to do', and Judas went off to betray him. It was night, the day for working had run out, the time for working freely was gone. In St John's Gospel, Jesus is tied up immediately. (There is no tying up in Luke and in Mark and Matthew until after he is found guilty of blasphemy.)

Jesus is now powerless. Pilate said to him, 'Do you know that I have power to crucify you and power to release you?' Jesus said 'You would have no power over me were it not given to you from above'. Jesus who had claimed power to judge, power over all flesh, is now under the power of pagan Rome.

One of the most moving examples of the change in the fortunes of Jesus (after the betrayal) is found in his terrible cry from the cross: 'I thirst.' We are reminded of an earlier time in the Gospel when Jesus cried out: 'He who believes in me shall never thirst.' 'If anyone thirsts let him come to me.' But now, he who would ease the thirst of the world was crying out for a drop of water. It was indeed a 'handing over'.

Let us now bring ourselves, our own lives, into the picture. Most people live an active life. They choose a vocation, they get married or they enter the religious life, they get a job, they run a business, they run a home, they make endless decisions. They control their immediate destiny, perhaps the destiny of many other people. In a word, they are 'in charge' – the subject of the sentence – as was the Lord in St Mark. They have power, they control, they act freely, as the Lord in St John.

Then a change takes place, a 'handing over'. Not a betrayal, but a very definite reversal. Nothing is the same again. This change can take many forms. It may be an accident or a heart attack. One passes into the hands of others, one is lifted by the crew of an ambulance, taken to hospital, examined, monitored, sustained by a drip, visited by friends. Everything is 'done' to one, happens to one.

Or retirement arrives. One is no longer in charge. You get the pension, are provided for. A profound change of consciousness takes place. You have to wait on the convenience of others. For some, this is a traumatic experience.

Or old age arrives. Time takes its time, but we all become old in the end. It can be very gradual, sometimes imperceptible. Then, as the poet says, 'And suddenly it is evening'. Things then are really never the same again.

So here we have two patterns or pictures, one in the life of Jesus and the reflection in our own lives. Thinking and praying as a Christian, I would have little doubt that the experience of the Lord was meant to light up and lighten our lot. It can, for example, be a great comfort and support to us in our sufferings to recall that Jesus suffered too, was in agony and fear. Sometimes a person will say in their plight 'Jesus knows all about it' – though we must not forget that this connection of our pain with that of the Lord may be only emotional. One could, if need be, replace the memory of the suffering Messiah with that of some saintly or revered figure who walked in suffering too. I recall a devout old lady finding comfort in the fact that her beloved mother suffered in the same way as herself. However, if it helps, it helps.

Then there is a second way of relating our handing over, our sufferings, to those of the Lord. It looks a simple way, but with a little thought and prayer can lead to a deep understanding. It begins with looking at the sufferings of Jesus, in his passion and death, and seeing it all as a sad end. ('It has all come to this.') He was in the end betrayed, abandoned, reduced to dying – as we all are.

But were the sufferings of Jesus a sad event? Had it all come to this? It had not. If we look closely at the manner in which

Jesus 'passed over' in his sufferings, we will see that his sufferings are never presented as a misfortune, but rather as a triumph. Nowhere is failure mentioned. Take Mark's centurion. He said: 'Truly this man was a son of God.' There was nothing in the Lord's sufferings, nothing in his reactions, nothing at all to incite the centurion to his declaration – but there was the belief of Mark that the sufferings of Jesus were a decisive manifestation of his divinity. At the forefront of his Gospel, Mark had written : 'The beginning of the Gospel of Jesus Christ, the Son of God'. He repeats it here at the end. We are not talking about failure; we are talking about triumph.

In St John, after the 'handing over' and through his sufferings, we have something more than triumph. We have achievement. At the Last Supper, Jesus prayed: 'I have completed the work you gave me to do.' But on the cross, it is final. He said 'It is finished'. According to St John, the Passion of Jesus is not human misfortune but the completion of the divine mission for which he came into the world.

Finally, and special to St John, there is something more than triumph and achievement in the story of Holy Week. There is glory. 'Glorification' is a great word in St John – 'Father, glorify thy name', and the answering 'I have glorified it and will glorify it again'. At the tomb of Lazarus, Martha is told that she will see the glory of God. But why then do we not (in St John) have the great scene of glory, the Transfiguration? We do have it, but at the handing over in Gethsemane. When Jesus meets the soldiers in the Garden and addresses them with the words 'I am He' they fall stunned to the ground. 'It is as Jesus is handed over … that the ultimate dimension of the Divine Glory becomes manifest in him and evident to all' (Vanstone).

So, in the light of all this – the Lord's achievement, triumph and glory in his 'handing over' – what about ourselves in sickness, in old age, in death? Can we not be inspired and challenged by his memory? Can we not find in our sufferings something of his triumph and achievement in our patience, acceptance, courage and hope? Can our end not be our transfiguration? And what a marvellous experience it is to witness people in old age or in pain being cheerful, accepting and appreciative. It is often a memorable and moving point in literature, as Malcolm said of Cawdor (in *Macbeth*): 'Nothing in his life became him like the leaving it. He died as one that had been studied in his death.' We are studied in our death through the memory and saving achievement of the dying Christ upon the cross.

There is, lastly, a third and most profound way in which we, in our sufferings and our end, can relate to the sufferings and end of Jesus' earthly life. We live in a particular kind of world. Its attitudes, assumptions and culture say certain things. One of them is that man's and woman's proper function is identified almost exclusively with action, with 'doing'. Human dignity and value, the culture says, are preserved only to the extent that we work, act, earn, achieve. There are many reasons for this, though some of them are not rooted in human nature itself.

However, these attitudes are there and they are very real. We compliment the elderly on being active. The elderly themselves are very anxious to claim that they 'can manage for themselves'. We praise them ('Isn't she great, now, really?'). You find people in retirement claiming that they are 'busier than ever'. You even find them (in normal times self-sufficient and indifferent to the comments of others) easily pleased or affronted by the remarks or comments of their friends.

But what did Jesus in his Passion say about this? He said, in effect, that we are deeply mistaken to think that we should always be 'doing', always managing for ourselves, always 'busier than ever'. The God revealed in Christ actually thought very differently. He had made the world. It was totally subject to him and yet, by the way he acted he gave to the world, to countless small things, an importance and a meaning they would otherwise never have had. He did, in fact, confer a final glory on creation and did it by submitting to the small things: letting himself be helped, be comforted by friends, receive a supportive hand, a drink, an anointing, a grave.

And so can we: while keeping in mind that it is good to be self-helping and active, we are most deeply one with the dying Christ when we allow people to help us, when we appreciate the kindness of nurse and doctor, when we welcome the person who brings our tray, the person who cleans the room, the friends who send cards or letters. We then share with Jesus the ultimate gesture of giving a meaning to all things great and small; and giving a special place to pain, retirement and old age.

We pray, Lord, this day, perhaps it is the evening of a day! Into all our lives will come 'the handing over' – of illness, accident, retirement, old age. May this moment of handing over be our moment of triumph and glory. Give us the spirit of acceptance, a willingness to accept the help of, have an appreciation of, the countless little things by which those who care for us help us. Let us join the good Lord in his final crowning of creation by giving a meaning to a cup of tea, a visit, a word, a helping hand and, finally, farewell.